The Art of Poetry volume 21

EDUQAS poetry anthology, *2025 onwards*

Published by Peripeteia Press Ltd.

First published: February 2025

ISBN: 978-1-913577-91-9

Peripeteia.co.uk

Contents

'How can the bird that is born for joy
Sit in a cage and sing?'

General Introduction to the *The Art of Poetry* series

The philosopher Nietzsche described his work as 'the greatest gift that [mankind] has ever been given'. The Elizabethan poet Edmund Spenser hoped his epic, 'The Faerie Queene', would magically transform its readers into noblemen. In comparison, our aims for 'The Art of Poetry' series of books are a tad more modest. Fundamentally we aim to provide books that will be of maximum use to English students and to their teachers.

In our experience, few students actually read essays on poems or any other form of literature, yet, whatever specification they are studying, they have to write analytical essays on poetry. So, we've offering some models, written in a lively, accessible and, we hope, engaging style. These are not intended as exemplars of exam style essays. Rather they demonstrate what high level, well informed, astute close reading of poetry looks like in essay form.

We believe that the essay as an art form needs demonstrating and championing, especially as so many revision books for students present information in broken down easy-to-digest note form. We would like to promote more sustained and demanding reading practice and hope our book will inspire students to write their own great essays, with the aim, of course, of reaching the very highest grades.

How to analyse a poem [seen or unseen]

A list of ingredients, not a recipe

Firstly, what not to do: sometimes pupils have been so programmed to spot poetic features such as alliteration that they start their analysis of a poem with close reading of these micro aspects of technique. This is never a good idea, because it divorces technique from themes and feelings. A far better strategy is to begin by trying to develop an overall understanding of what you think the poem is about. Once you've established the central concerns, you can delve into the poem's interior, examining its inner workings. And you should always be flexible enough to adapt, refine or even reject your initial thoughts in the light of your close investigation. The essential thing is to make sure that whether you're discussing imagery or stanza form, sonic effects or syntax, enjambment or vocabulary, you always explore the significance of the feature in terms of meanings and effect.

Someone once compared texts to cakes. When you're presented with a cake the first thing you notice is what it looks like. Probably the next thing you'll do is taste it and find out if you like the flavour. This aesthetic experience will come first. Only later might you investigate the ingredients and how it was made. Adopting a uniform reading strategy is like a recipe; it sets out what you must, do step by step, in a predetermined order. This can be helpful, especially when you start reading and analysing poems. In our first volume in The Art of Poetry series, for example, we explored each poem under the same subheadings of narrator, characters, imagery, patterns of sound, form & structure and contexts, and all our essays followed essentially the same direction. Of course, this is a reasonable strategy for reading poetry and will stand you in good stead. However, this present volume takes a different, more flexible approach, because this book is designed for students aiming for levels 7 to 9, or A to A* in old currency, and to reach the highest levels your work needs to be a bit more conceptual, critical and individual. Writing frames for your essays are also useful for beginners, like stabilisers when you learn to ride a bike. But, if you wish to write top level essays you need to develop your own more individual ways of reading and your own essay frames.

Read our essays and you'll find that they all include the same principal ingredients – detailed, 'fine-grained' reading of crucial elements of poetry, imagery, form, rhyme and so forth – but each essay starts in a different way and each one has a slightly different focus or weight of attention on the various aspects that make up a poem. Once you feel you have mastered the apprentice strategy of reading all poems in the same way, we strongly recommend you put any generic essay recipe approach to one side and move on to a new way of reading, an approach that can change depending on the nature of the poem you're reading.

Follow your nose

Having established what you think a poem is about – its theme and what is interesting about the poet's treatment of the theme [the conceptual bit] – rather than then working through a pre-set agenda, decide what you honestly think are the most interesting aspects of the poem and start analysing these carefully. This way your response will be original [a key marker of a top band essay] and you'll be writing about material you find most interesting. In other words, you're foregrounding yourself as an individual, critical reader. These most interesting aspects might be ideas or technique based, or both, or better style explore how techniques are used to communicate thematic ideas.

Follow your own, informed instincts, trust in your own critical intelligence as a reader. If you're writing about material that genuinely interests you, your writing is likely to be interesting for the examiner too. And, obviously, take advice to from your teacher too, use their expertise and, when you can, read what other intelligent readers have written.

Because of the focus on sonic effects such as alliteration and on imagery other aspects of poems are often overlooked by students. It is a rare student, for instance, who notices how punctuation works in a poem and who can write about it convincingly. Few students write about the contribution of the unshowy function words, such as pronouns, prepositions or conjunctions, yet these words are crucial to any text. Of course, it would be a highly risky strategy to focus your whole essay on a seemingly innocuous and incidental detail of a poem. But coming at things from an unusual angle is as important to writing great essays as it is to the production of great poetry.

So, in summary, when reading a poem for the first time, such as when doing an 'unseen' style question, have a check list in mind, but don't feel you must follow someone else's generic essay recipe. Don't feel that you must always start with a consideration of imagery if the poem you're analysing has, for instance, an eye-catching form. Consider the significance of major features, such as imagery, vocabulary, sonic patterns and form, but, crucially, try to write about these aspects in terms of their significance, their contribution to themes and effects. But also follow your nose, find your own direction, seek out aspects that genuinely engage you and write about these.

The essays in this volume provide examples and we hope they will encourage you to go your own way, at least to some extent, and to make discoveries for yourself. No single essay could possibly cover everything that could be said about any one of these poems; aiming to create comprehensive essays like this would be utterly foolish. And we have not tried to do so. Nor are our essays meant to be models for exam essays – they're far too long for that. They do, however, illustrate the sort of conceptualised, critical and 'fine-grained' exploration demanded for top grades at GCSE and beyond. There's always more to be discovered, more to say, space in other words for you to develop some original reading of your own, space for you to write your own individual essay recipe.

Writing literature essays

The Big picture and the small

An essay itself can be a form of art. Writing a great essay takes time, skill and practice. Expert advice is always helpful. Study the two figures in the picture carefully and describe what you can see. Channel your inner Sherlock Holmes to add any deductions you are able to form about the image. Before reading what we have to say, write your description out as a prose paragraph. Probably you'll have written something along the following lines:

First off, the overall impression: this picture is very blurry. Probably this indicates that either this is a very poor-quality reproduction, or that it is a copy of a very small detail from a much bigger image that has been magnified several times. The image shows a stocky man and a medium-sized dog, both orientated towards something to their left, which suggests there is some point of interest in that direction. From the man's rustic dress (smock, breeches, clog-like boots) the picture is either an old one or a modern one depicting the past. The man appears to be carrying a stick and there's maybe a bag on his back. From all of these details we can probably deduce that he's a peasant, maybe a farmer or a shepherd.

Now do the same thing for picture two. We have even less detail here and again the picture's blurry. Particularly without the benefit of colour, it's hard to determine what we're seeing other than a horizon and maybe the sky. We might just be able to make out that in the centre of the picture is the shape of the sun. From the reflection, we can deduce that the image is of the sun either setting or rising over water. If it is dawn this usually symbolises hope, birth and new beginnings; if the sun is setting it conventionally symbolises the opposite – the end of things, the coming of night/ darkness, death.

If you're a sophisticated reader, you might well start to think about links between the two images. Are they, perhaps, both details from the same single larger image, for instance. And what about the image below? This

may be even harder to work out. Now we don't even have a whole figure. Is that a leg perhaps and a foot stick out and upwards? Whatever is happening her, it looks painful and we can't see the torso or head, which may be submerged beneath water perhaps. From the upside-down orientation, we might surmise that the figure has fallen, possibly into the sea or a lake. If we put this image with the one above, we might decide that the figure has, indeed, fallen into water as there are horizontal marks on the image that could be splashes. From the quality of this image we can deduce that this is an even smaller detail blown-up.

By now, you may be wondering why we've suddenly moved into rudimentary art appreciation. On the other hand, you may already have worked out the point of this exercise. Either way, bear with us, because this is the last picture for you to describe and analyse. So, what have we here? Looks like another peasant, again from the past, perhaps medieval (?) from the smock-like dress, clog-like shoes and the britches. This character is also probably male and seems to be pushing some wooden apparatus from left to right. From the ridges at the bottom left of the image we can guess that he's working the land, probably driving a plough. Noticeably the figure has his back to us; we see he is turned

away from us, suggesting his whole concentration is on the task at hand. In the background appear to be sheep, which would fit with our impression that this is an image of farming. It seems likely that this image and the first one come from the same painting. They have a similar style and subject and it is possible that these sheep belong to our first character. This image is far less blurry than the other one. Either it is a better-quality reproduction, or this is a larger, more significant detail extracted from the original source. If this is a significant detail, it's interesting that we cannot see the character's face. From this we can deduce that he's not important in and of himself; rather he's a representative figure and the important thing is what he is and what he isn't looking at.

Okay, we hope we haven't stretched your patience too far. What's the point of all this? Well, let's imagine we prefixed the paragraphs above with an introduction, along the following lines: 'The painter makes this picture interesting and powerful by using several key techniques and details' and that we added a conclusion, along the lines of 'So now I have shown how the painter has made this picture interesting and powerful through the use of a number of key techniques and details'. Finally, substitute painter and picture for writer and text. If we put together our paragraphs into an essay what would be its strengths and weaknesses? And what might be a better approach to writing our essay?

Consider the strengths first off: The best bits of our essay, we humbly suggest, are where we begin to explain what we are seeing, when we do the Holmes like deductive thinking. Another strength might be that we have started to make links between the various images, or parts of a larger image, to see how they work together to provide us more information. A corresponding weakness is that each of our paragraphs seems like a separate chunk of writing. The weaker parts of the paragraphs are where we simply describe what we can see. More importantly though, if we used our comments on image one as our first paragraph we seem to have started in a rather random way. Why should we have begun our essay with that particular image? What was the logic behind that? And most importantly of all, if this image is an analogue for a specific technique in a text, such as a poem's alliteration or a novel's dialogue, we have plunged into analysing this technical aspect before we're established any overall sense of the painting/ text. This is a very common fault with GCSE English Literature essays. As we've said before and will keep saying, pupils start writing detailed micro-analysis of a feature such as alliteration before they have established the big picture of what the text is about and what the answer to the question they've been set might be. Without this big picture it's very difficult to write about the significance of these micro details. And the highest marks for English essays are reserved for explanations of the significance and effects generated by a writer's craft.

Now we'll try a different and much better approach. Let's start off with the big picture, the whole image. The painting on the next page is called *Landscape with the fall of Icarus*. It's usually attributed to the Renaissance artist, Pieter Breughel and was probably painted in the 1560s. Icarus is a character from Greek mythology. He was the son of the brilliant inventor, Daedalus. Trapped on Crete by the evil King Minos, Daedalus and Icarus managed to escape when the inventor created pairs of giant feathered wings. Before they took to sky Daedalus warned his son not to get too excited and fly too near the sun as the wings were held together by wax that might melt. Icarus didn't listen, however. The eventual result was that he plummeted back to earth, into the sea, and was killed.

Applying this contextual knowledge to the painting, we can see that the image is about how marginal Icarus' tragedy is in the big picture. Conventionally we'd expect any image depicting such a famous myth to make Icarus's fall the dramatic focal point. The main objects of this painting, however, are emphatically not the very small image of the falling boy hitting the water. Instead, our eye is drawn to the peasant in the centre of the painting, pushing his plough (even more so in colour as his shirt is the only red object in an otherwise greeny-yellow landscape) and the stately galleon sailing calmly past those protruding legs.

Seeing the whole image, we can appreciate the significance of the shepherd and the ploughman looking up and down and to the left. The point being made is how they don't even notice the tragedy because they have work to do and need to get on with their lives. The animals too seem unconcerned. As W. H. Auden's puts it, in lines from his poem Musée des Beaux Arts, 'everything turns away / Quite leisurely from the disaster'.

To sum up, when writing an essay on any literary text do not begin with close-up analysis of micro-details. Begin instead with establishing the whole picture: What the text is about, what key techniques the writer uses, when it was written, what sort of text it is, what effects it has on the reader. Then, when you zoom in to examine smaller details, such as imagery, individual words, metre or sonic techniques, discuss these in relation to their significance in terms of this bigger picture.

What would our art appreciation essay look like now?

Paragraph #1: Introduction – myth of Icarus, date of painting, the way our eyes are drawn away from his tragic death to much more ordinary life going around him. Significance of this – even tragic suffering goes on around us without us even noticing because we're too busy getting on with our lives.

Paragraph #2: We could, of course, start with our first figure and follow the same order as we've presented the images here. But wouldn't it make more logical sense to discuss the biggest, more prominent images in the painting first? So, our first paragraph is about the ploughman and his horse. How his figure placed centrally and is bent downwards towards the ground and turned left away from us etc.

Paragraph #3: The next most prominent image is the ship. Also moving from right to left, as if the main point of interest in the painting is off in that direction. Here we could consider the other human agricultural figure, the shepherd and his dog and, of course, the equally oblivious sheep.

Paragraph #4: Having moved on to examining background details in the painting we could discuss the symbolism of the sun on the horizon. While this could be the sun rising, the context of the story suggests it is more likely to be setting. The pun of the sun/son going down makes sense.

Paragraph #5: Finally, we can turn our attention to the major historical and literary figure in this painting, Icarus and how he is presented. This is the key image in terms of understanding the painting's purpose and effect.

Paragraph #6: Conclusion. What is surprising about this picture? How do the choices the painter makes affect us as viewer/ reader? Does this painting make Icarus's story seem more pathetic, more tragic or something else?

Now, all you have to do is switch from a painting to a poem.

Big pictures, big cakes, recipes and lists of instructions; following your own nose and going your own way. Whatever metaphors we use, your task is to bring something personal and individual to your critical reading of poems and to your essay writing and always to write about the significance of features.

Writing comparative essays

The following is adapted from our discussion of this topic in 'The Art of Writing English Literature Essays' A-level course companion, and is a briefer version, tailored to the GCSE exam task. Fundamentally comparative essays want you to display not only your ability to intelligently write about literary texts, but also your ability to make meaningful connections between them. The first starting point is your topic. This must be broad enough to allow substantial thematic overlapping of the texts. However, too little overlap and it will be difficult to connect the texts; too much overlap and your discussion will be lopsided and one-dimensional. The exam question will ask you to focus on the methods used by the poets to explore how two poems present one of these themes. You will also be directed to write specifically on language and imagery [AO2] as well as on the contexts in which the poems were written [AO3].

One poem from the anthology will be specified and printed on the paper. You will then have to choose a companion poem. Selecting the right poem for interesting comparison is obviously very important. Obviously, you should prepare for this question beforehand by pairing up the poems, especially as you will only have about forty minutes to complete this task. You will also be asked to compare unseen poems, so grasping how best to write comparative essays is essential to your chance of reaching the top grades. To think about this task visually, you don't want Option A, below, [not enough overlap] or Option B [two much overlap]. You want Option C. This option allows substantial common links to be built between your chosen texts where discussion arises from both fundamental similarities AND differences.

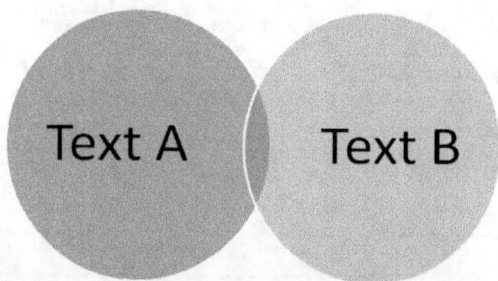

Option A: too many differences

Option B: too many similarities

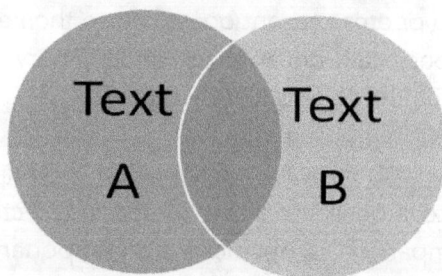

Option C: suitable number of similarities and differences

The final option will generate the most interesting discussion as it will allow substantial similarities to emerge as well as differences. The best comparative essays actually find that what seemed like clear similarities become subtle differences and vice versa while still managing to find rock solid similarities to build their foundations on.

Check the mark scheme for this question and you'll notice that to reach the top grade your comparison must be 'well-structured'. How should you structure a comparative essay? Consider the following alternatives. Which one is best and why?

Essay Structure #1
1. Introduction
2. Main body paragraph #1 - Text A
3. Main body paragraph #2 - Text A
4. Main body paragraph #3 - Text B
5. Main body paragraph #4 - Text B
6. Conclusion

Essay Structure #2
1. Introduction
2. Main body paragraph #1 - Text A
3. Main body paragraph #2 - Text A
4. Main body paragraph #3 - Text B
5. Main body paragraph #4 - Text B
6. Comparison of main body paragraphs #1 & #3 - Text A + B
7. Comparison of main body paragraphs #2 & #4 - Text A + B
8. Conclusion

Essay Structure #3
1. Introduction
2. Main body paragraph #1 - Text A + B
3. Main body paragraph #2 - Text A + B
4. Main body paragraph #3 - Text A + B
5. Main body paragraph #4 - Text A+ B
6. Conclusion

We hope you will agree that 3 is the optimum option. Option 1 is the dreaded 'here is everything I know about text A, followed by everything I know by Text B' approach where the examiner has to work out what the connections are between the texts. This will score the lowest marks. Option 2 is better: There is some attempt to compare the two texts.

However, it is a very inefficient way of comparing the two texts. For comparative essay writing the most important thing is to discuss both texts together. This is the most effective and efficient way of achieving your overall aim. Option 3 does this by comparing and contrasting the two texts under common umbrella headings. This naturally encourages comparison. Using comparative discourse markers, such as 'similarly', 'in contrast to', 'conversely' 'likewise' and 'however' also facilitates effective comparison.

When writing about each poem, make sure you do not work chronologically through a poem, summarising the content of each stanza. Responses of this sort typically start with 'In the first stanza' and employ discourse markers of time rather than comparison, such as 'after', 'next', 'then' and so forth. Even if your reading is analytical rather than summative, your essay should not work through the poem from the opening to the ending. Instead, make sure you write about the ideas explored in both texts (themes), the feelings and effects generated and the techniques the poets utilise to communicate these.

Writing about language

Poems are paintings as well as windows; we look at them as well as through them. As you know, special attention should be paid to language in poetry because of all the literary art forms poetry, in particular, employs language in a precise, self-conscious and distinctive way. Ideally in poetry, every word should count. Analysis of language falls into distinct categories:

- By **diction** we mean the vocabulary used in a poem. A poem might be composed from the ordinary language of everyday speech, or it might use elaborate, technical or elevated phrasing. Or both. At one time, some words and types of words were considered inappropriate for the rarefied field of poetry. The great Irish poet, W. B. Yeats never referred to modern technology in his poetry, there are no cars, or tractors or telephones, because he did not consider such things fitting for poetry. When much later, Philip Larkin used swear words in his otherwise well-mannered verse the effect was deeply shocking. Modern poets have pretty much dispensed with the idea of there being an elevated literary language appropriate for poetry. Hence in the Eduqas anthology you'll find all sorts of modern, everyday spoken language.

- **Grammatically** a poem may use complex or simple sentences (the key to which is the conjunctions); it might employ a wash of adjectives and adverbs, or it may rely extensively on the bare force of nouns and verbs. Picking out and exploring words from specific grammatical classes has the merit of being both incisive and usually illuminating.

- Poets might mix together different types, conventions and **registers** of language, moving, for example, between formal and informal, spoken and written, modern and archaic, and so forth. Arranging the diction in the poem in terms of **lexico-semantic** fields, by register or by etymology, helps reveal underlying patterns of meaning.

- For almost all poems **imagery** is a crucial aspect of language. Broadly imagery is a synonym for description and can be broken down into two types, **sensory** and **figurative.** Sensory imagery means the words and phrases that appeal to our senses, to touch and taste, hearing, smell and sight. Sensory imagery is evocative; it helps to take us into the world of the poem to share the experience being described. Figurative imagery, in particular, is always significant. As we have mentioned, not all poems rely on metaphors and similes; these devices are only part of a poet's box of tricks, but figurative language is always important when it occurs because it compresses multiple meanings into itself. To use a technical term figurative images are polysemic - they contain many meanings. Try writing out all the meanings contained in a metaphor in a more concise and economical way and you'll use more words than you started with. Even simple, everyday metaphors compress meaning. If, for example, we want to say our teacher is fierce and powerful and that we fear his or her wrath, we can more concisely say our teacher is a dragon.

Writing about patterns of sound

Like painters, some poets have powerful visual imaginations, while other poets have stronger auditory imaginations and are more like musicians. Some poems are like paintings, while others are more like pieces of music.

Firstly, what not to do: Tempting as it may be to spot sonic features of a poem and list these, don't do this. Avoid something along the lines of 'The poet uses alliteration here and the rhyme scheme is ABABCDCDEFEFGG'. Sometimes, indeed, it may be tempting to set out the poem's whole rhyme scheme like this. Resist the temptation: This sort of identification of features is worth zero marks. Marks in exams are reserved for attempts to link techniques to meanings and to effects, to what is significant.

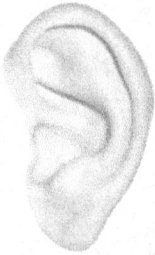

Probably many of us have been sitting in English lessons listening somewhat sceptically as our English teacher explains the surprisingly specific significance of a seemingly random piece of alliteration in a poem. Something along the lines 'The double d sounds here reinforce a sense of invincible strength' or 'the harsh repetition of the 't' sounds suggests anger'. Through all our minds at some point may have passed the idea that, in these instances, English teachers appear to be using some sort of Enigma-style secret symbolic decoding machine that reveals how particular patterns of sounds have such definite encoded meanings.

And this sort of thing is not all nonsense. Originally deriving from an oral tradition, most poems are, of course, written for the ear as much as for the eye, to be heard as much as read. A poem is a soundscape as much as it is a set of meanings. Sounds are, however, difficult to tie to very definite meanings and effects. By way of example, the old BBC Radiophonic workshop, which produced ambient sounds for radio and television programmes, used the same sound in different contexts, knowing that the audience would perceive them in the appropriate way because of that context. Hence the sound effect of bacon sizzling, of an audience clapping and of feet walking over gravel were actually recordings of an identical sound. Listeners heard them differently because of the context they were placed in, a kitchen, a performance and so forth. So, we may, indeed, be able to spot the repeated 's' sounds in a poem, but whether this creates a hissing sound, yes like a snake, or the susurration of the sea will depend on the context within the poem and the ears of the reader. Whether a sound is soft and soothing or harsh and grating is also open to interpretation.

The idea of connecting these sounds to meanings or significance is a productive one. And your analysis will be most convincing if you use several pieces of evidence together. In other words, rather than try to pick out individual examples of sonic effects, we recommend you explore the weave or pattern of sounds, the effects these generate and their contribution to feelings and ideas. For example, this might mean examining how alliteration and assonance are used together to achieve a particular mimetic effect.

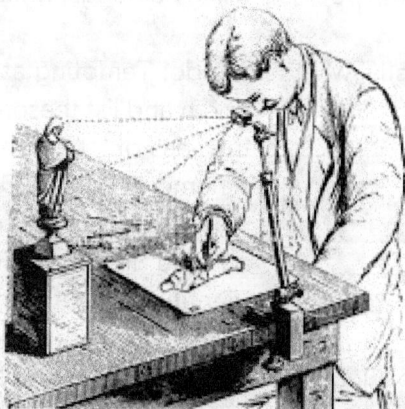

Writing about form & structure

As you know, there are no marks for simply identifying textual features. This holds true for language, sounds and also for form and structure. Consider instead the relationship between a poem's form, structure and its content, themes and effects.

There is no exact distinction between the two terms, form and structure. For example, the structural feature of stanzas is referred to technically as stanza form. So there is overlap in meaning between the two words. However, this doesn't mean they are exactly the same. A useful way to conceptualise the distinction between them is to use the metaphor of a building. The form of a building is whether it is a house, a school, a hospital, while the walls, floors, roof etc. are its structural features. Or switch the metaphor to vehicles and the form might a car, or a bus, or a lorry, and the structure, the panels, the suspension, wheels, bonnet etc. If we switch back to poetry, the type of poem, such a sonnet is the form. This form is constructed through structural elements, such as a rhyme scheme, a metre, a set number of lines and usually an arrangement of two stanzas into an octave and a sestet.

A poem's form can be closed, open or free. Closed forms, such as the sonnet have a set number of lines as well as rhyme scheme, stanza form and metre. Open forms, such as ballads, have the latter three but not a set number of lines. Free forms dispense with all of these features. Poems can also be arranged on a spectrum from highly regular, such as closed forms, to highly
irregular, such as free verse forms.

When writing about structure, consider the following aspects of a poem:

1. Lineation – is there a regular line length? If so, what is the principle controlling this? The number of syllables, beats, words?
2. Metre – Is there a regular metre, such as an iambic pentameter? Or an irregular metre or no metre at all?
3. Stanzas – Are the stanzas regular, such as each one being a quatrain, or are they varied? Are the stanzas connected or

separate? What is the relationship between the stanzas?

4. Rhyme – Is there a regular rhyme scheme with rhymes at the ends of lines or a more irregular scheme or no rhyme at all?

5. Caesura and enjambment. Caesuras break lines of verse and are usually indicated by a full stop or colon, whereas enjambment links lines together by making sentences flow over from one line to the next. The opposite of enjambment is called end-stopping, where a sentence ends at the end of a line.

Other elements in a poem that can be analysed through structure include syntax (the word order in sentences), the handling of time and the arrangement of narrative.

The key idea to grasp is that form and structure are not merely decorative or ornamental: A poem's meanings and effects are generated through the interplay of form, structure and content. Broadly speaking the form and structure can either work with or against a poem's content. Conventionally a sonnet, for instance, is about love, whereas a limerick is a comic form. A serious love poem in the form of a limerick would be unusual, as would a sonnet about an old man with a beard.

Sometimes poetic form and structure can create an ironic backdrop to highlight an aspect of content. An example would be a formally elegant

poem about something monstrous, or a fragile form containing something robust. Wilfred Owen's famous double sonnet, *Dulce et Decorum Est* might spring to mind. The visual artist Grayson Perry often uses form in this ironic way. Rather than depicting the sort of picturesque, idealised images we expect of ceramics, Perry's pots and urns frequently depict modern life in bright, garish colours. The urn pictured, for instance, is entitled *Modern Family* and depicts two gay men with a boy who they have presumably adopted. A thrash metal concert inside a church, a philosophical essay via text message, a fine crystal goblet filled with fizzy pop would be further examples of ironic relationships between message and medium, content and context or form and structure.

Reading form & structure

Put a poem before your eyes. Start off taking a panoramic perspective: Think of the forest, not the trees. Perhaps mist over your eyes a bit. Don't even read the words, just look at the poem, like at a painting. Is the poem slight, thin, fat, long, short? What is the relation of whiteness to blackness? Why might the poet have chosen this shape? Does it look regular or irregular? A poem about a long winding river will probably look rather different from one about a small pebble or should do. Unless form is being employed ironically. Now read the poem a couple of times. First time, fast as you can, second time more slowly and carefully. How does the visual layout of the poem relate to what it seems to be about? Does this form support, or create a tension against, the content? Is the form one you recognise, like a sonnet, or is it more open, more irregular like free verse? Usually, the latter is obvious from the irregularity of the stanzas, line lengths and lack of metre or rhyme.

As Hurley and O'Neill explain in 'Poetic Form: An Introduction', like genre, form sets expectations: 'In choosing form, poets bring into play associations and expectations which they may then satisfy, modify or subvert'.[1] We've already suggested that if we see a poem is a sonnet or a limerick this recognition will set up expectations about the nature of the poem's content. The same thing works on a smaller level; once we have noticed that a poem's first stanza is a quatrain, we expect it to continue in this neat, orderly fashion. If the quatrain's rhyme scheme is xaxa, xbxb, in which only the second and fourth lines rhyme, we expect that the next stanza will be xcxc. So, if it isn't we need to consider why.

After taking in the big picture in terms of choice of form in relation to content zoom in: Explore the stanza form, lineation, punctuation, the use of enjambment and caesura. Single line stanzas draw attention to themselves. If they are end-stopped, they can suggest isolation, separation. Couplets imply twoness. Stanzas of three lines are called tercets and feature in villanelles and terza rima. On the page, both these

---

[1] Hurley & O'Neill, 'Poetic Form, An Introduction', p.3.

forms tend to look rather delicate, especially if separated from each other by the silence of white space. Often balanced through rhyme, quatrains look a bit more robust and sturdier. Cinquains are swollen quatrains in which the last line often seems to throw the stanza a little out of kilter.

Focus in on specific examples and on points of transition. For instance, if a poem has four regular quatrains followed by a couplet, examine the effect of this change. If we've been ticking along nicely in iambic metre and suddenly trip on a trochee, examine why. Consider regularity. Closed forms of poems, such as villanelles, are highly regular with set rhyme schemes, metre and number of lines. In free verse poems, the poet dispenses with any set metre, rhyme scheme or recognisable traditional form. What stops this sort of poetry from merely being prose chopped up to look like verse? The care of the design on the page. Hence, in free verse poems we need to focus more intently on lineation. Enjambment runs over lines and makes connections; caesura pauses a line and separates words. Lots of enjambment generates a sense of the language running away from the speaker. Lots of caesuras generate a halting, hesitant, choppy movement to lines. Opposites, these devices work in tandem and where they fall is always significant in a good poem.

Remember, a poem's form and the underpinning structure is never merely decorative. And bear in mind too the fact that the most volatile materials require the strongest containers.

Nice to metre...
A brief guide to metre and rhythm in poetry

Why express yourself in poetry? Why read words dressed up and expressed as a poem? What can you get from poetry that you can't from prose? There are many compelling answers to these questions. Here, though, we're going to concentrate on one aspect of the unique appeal of poetry – the structure of sound. Whatever our stage of education, we are all already sophisticated at detecting and using structured sound. Try reading the following sentences without any variation whatsoever in how each sound is emphasised, and they will quickly lose what essential human characteristics they have. The sentences will sound robotic. So, in a sense, we won't be teaching anything new here. It's just that in poetry the structure of sound is unusually crafted and carefully created. It becomes a key part of what a poem is.

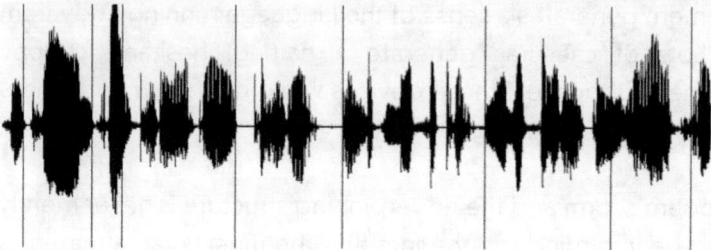

We will introduce a few new key technical terms along the way, but the ideas are straightforward. Individual sounds (syllables) are either stressed so that they sound louder and longer or unstressed. As well as clustering into words and sentences for meaning, these sounds cluster into rhythmic groups or feet, producing the poem's metre, which is the characteristic way its rhythm works.

In some poems, the rhythm is very regular and may even have a name, such as iambic pentameter. At the other extreme, a poem may have no discernible regularity at all. As we have said, this is called free verse. It is vital to remember that the sound in a good poem is structured so that it combines effectively with the meanings.

For example, take a look at these two lines from Andrew Marvell's famous poem *To his Coy Mistress*:

'But at my back I alwaies hear
Times winged Chariot hurrying near:'

Forgetting the rhythms for a moment, Marvell is basically saying at this point 'Life is short, Time flies, and it's after us'. Now concentrate on the rhythm of his words.

- In the first line every other syllable is stressed: 'at', 'back', 'al', 'hear'.
- Each syllable before these is unstressed 'But', 'my', 'I', 'aies'.
- This is a regular beat or rhythm which we could write
  ti TUM / ti TUM / ti TUM / ti TUM , with the / separating the feet. ('Feet' is the technical term for metrical units of sound).
- This type of two beat metrical pattern is called iambic, and because there are four feet in the line, this example is tetrameter. So this line is in 'iambic tetrameter'. (Tetra is Greek for four.)
- Notice that 'my' and 'I' being unstressed diminishes the speaker, and we are already prepared for what is at his 'back', what he can 'hear' to be bigger than him, since these sounds are stressed.
- On the next line, the iambic rhythm is immediately broken off, since the next line hits us with two consecutive stressed syllables straight off: 'Times' 'wing'. Because a pattern had been established, when it suddenly changes the reader feels it, the words feel crammed together more urgently, the beats of the rhythm are closer, some little parcels of time have gone missing.

A physical rhythmic sensation is created of time slipping away, running out. This subtle sensation is enhanced by the stress-unstress-unstress pattern of words that follow, 'chariot hurrying' (TUM-ti-ti, TUM-ti-ti). So, in short, the hurrying sounds underscore the meaning of the words.

Scansion

The term 'scansion' refers to working out the metrical pattern of a poem, if there is a metrical pattern. Sometimes teachers shy away from this exercise because they fear it will encourage pupils to simply identify technical features, such as iambic pentameter, rather than analysing their significance.

There are two key ideas you need to understand about scansion:

1. Scansion is a type of interpretation
2. Poems may have a dominant metre, but there will be variations, and these variations are always significant.

1.

Scansion is to some extent a type of interpretation. While in some poems and certainly in some lines within poems the metre will be very distinct and not a matter for debate, in most poems and many lines there will be several different ways the metrics could be scanned.

In his excellent poetry primer, 'The Ode Less Travelled', Stephen Fry gives an example of a line with a distinct metre:

'He bangs the drum and makes a noise.'

Clearly this is iambic tetrameter, with strong stresses on the important words, 'bangs', 'drum', 'makes' and 'noise'. All the unstressed syllables are function words, 'he', 'the', 'and' and 'a'.
So that the line can be scanned as:

'He **bangs** the **drum** and **makes** a **noise**'

In this case, it isn't a matter of interpretation as the pattern is distinct. That said, it is possible that in a particular context where the maleness of the drum banger is significant that the first syllable could then be stressed.

In contrast to the pronounced pattern above, where there a clear strong and weak stresses would be a line such as Shakespeare's opening one to sonnet 18:

'Shall I compare thee to a summer's day?'

This line could be scanned as regular iambic pentameter:

'Shall **I** com**pare** thee **to** a **sum**mer's **day**?'

But what if the question is more about whether to do this rather than whether the speaker should make the comparison? If that's the case, then the stresses in the first two words, the first metrical foot, are the other way round – '**Shall** I...' As actors know from reading Shakespeare's lines in his plays, small shifts in emphasis can subtly change the meaning of the words. So too is the case in poetry.

Here's another example, the opening line of Wilfred Owen's *Dulce et Decorum Est*:
'Bent double, like old beggars under sacks'

This could be scanned a regular iambic pentameter:

'Bent **double**, **like** old **beg**gars **under** **sacks**'

Maybe that's right, but the problem with that scansion is that it emphasises a relatively unimportant word, 'like', at the expense of seemingly more important words, such as 'bent' and 'old'. An alternative scansion of the lines would be:

'**Bent double**, like **old beg**gars **under sacks**'

While this is still a pentameter, now we have two successive strong stresses, a spondee, at the start and again in the middle of the line and a little run of two unstressed syllables. This more lumpen pattern seems truer to what Owen is describing. That the young men have been prematurely aged by war is surely significant - hence the adjective 'old' has to take a stress. Not everyone might agree. Hence scansion is, to some degree, a matter of interpretation.

2.

When we say a poem has a particular metre, such as iambic pentameter, it means the majority, but not all the lines, fall into that pattern. There will be some small variations in this dominant pattern, and, if the poem's a good one, these variations will be significant. A poem in which every line followed exactly the same metre would, in fact, sound mechanical, even robotic. Moreover, subtly, sonically, variations in the metre, draw our attention to words that don't quite fit, either quickening or slowing the reading process down, as in the examples quoted in the previous section.

In William Blake's poem *The Tyger*, for example, most of the lines are written in trochaic tetrameter, so this is the dominant metre of the poem. Here's the famous first line:

'Tyger, Tyger, **burn**ing **bright**'

But this pattern reverses in the line in which the tyger is brought to life, thus mimicking its heartbeat:

'And **when** thy **heart** be**gan** to **beat**'

If you establish the dominant metre, focus then on where the poem slips out of this metre, even momentarily. Don't assume this is a mistake, due a lack of metrical skill by the poet. Assume it is a deliberate choice. Then consider why the poet might have made this choice.

14 ways of looking at a poem

Though conceived as pre-reading exercises, most of these tasks work just as well for revision.

1. Mash them (1) – mix together lines from two or more poems. The students' task is to untangle the poems from each other.

2. Mash them (2) – the second time round make the task significantly harder. Rather than just mixing whole lines, mash the poems together more thoroughly, words, phrases, images and all, so that unmashing seems impossible. At first sight at least.

3. Dock the last stanza or few lines from a poem. The students should come up with their own endings for the poem. Then compare theirs with the poet's version. Or present the poem without its title. Can the students come up with a suitable one?

4. Break a poem into segments. Split the class into groups. Each group work in isolation on their segment and feedback on what they discover. Then their task is to fit the poem and their ideas about it together as a whole.

5. Give the class the first and last stanza of a poem. Their task is to provide the filling. They can choose to attempt the task at beginner level (in prose) or at world class level

    (in poetry).

6. Add superfluous words to a poem. Start off with obvious interventions, such as the interjection of blatantly alien, noticeable words. Try smuggling 'pineapple', 'bourbon' and 'haberdashers' into any of the poems and see if you can get it past the critical sensors.

7. Repeat the exercise – This time using much less extravagant

words. Try to smuggle in a few intensifiers, such as 'really', 'very' and 'so'. Or extra adjectives.

8. Collapse the lineation in a poem and present it as continuous prose. The students' task is to put it back into verse. Discussing the various pros and cons or various possible arrangements – short lines, long lines, irregular lines - can be very productive. Pay particular attention to line breaks and the words that end them. After a whatever-time-you- deem-fit, give the class the pattern of the first stanza. They then have to decide how to arrange the next stanza. Drip feed the rest of the poem to them.

9. Find a way to present the shapes of each poem on the page without the words. The class should work through each poem, two minutes at a time, speculating on what the shape might tell us about the content of the poem. This exercise works especially well as a starter activity. We recommend you use two poems at a time, as the comparison helps students to recognise and appreciate different shapes.

10. Test the thesis that an astute reader can recognise poems by men from those written by women. Give the class one of the poems without the name of the poet. Ask them to identify whether the writer is male or female and to explain their reasons for identifying them as such. Or switch all the pronouns in a poem from male to female or vice versa. What is the effect?

11. Split the class into groups. Each group should focus their analysis on a different feature of the poem. Start with the less obvious aspects: Group 1 should concentrate on enjambment and caesuras; group 2 on punctuation; group 3 on the metre and rhythm; group 4 on function words – conjunctions, articles, prepositions. 2-5 mins. only. Then swap focus, four times. Share findings.

12. In 'Observations on Poetry', Robert Graves wrote that 'rhymes properly used are the good servants whose presence at the dinner-table gives the guests a sense of opulent security; never

awkward or over-clever, they hand the dishes silently and professionally. You can trust them not to interrupt the conversation or allow their personal disagreements to come to the notice of the guests; but some of them are getting very old for their work'. Explore the poets' use of rhyme in the light of Graves' comment. Are the rhymes ostentatiously original or old hat? Do they stick out of the poem or are they neatly tucked in? Are they dutiful servants of meaning or noisy disrupters of the peace?

13. The Romantic poet, John Keats, claimed that 'we hate poetry that has a palpable design upon us'. Apply his comment to this selection of poems. Do any seem to have a 'palpable design' on the reader? If so, how does the poet want us to respond?

14. Each student should crunch the poem down to one word per line. Discuss this process as a class. Project the poem so the whole class can see it and start the crunching process by indicating and then crossing-out the function words from each line. Now discuss which of the remaining words is most important. This will also give you an opportunity to refer to grammatical terms, such as nouns and verbs. Once each line has been reduced to one word, from this list, pupils should crunch again. This time all that should remain are the five most important words in the whole poem. Now they need to write two or three sentences for each of these words explaining exactly why they are so important and why the poet didn't choose any of the possible synonyms.

'Poetry is only there to frame the silence. There is silence between each verse and silence at the end.'

ALICE OSWALD

William Blake, *The Schoolboy*

Clumsily amateurish or the real thing?

Try to work out the metrical arrangement of Blake's impassioned dramatic monologue and you'll soon discover it seems to be all over the place. Granted, the first line is reasonably regular, an iambic tetrameter that establishes a song-like form:

'I **love** to **rise** in a **sum**mer **morn**'

Even here, though, there's a little extra unstressed syllable between **'rise'** and **'sum'**, suitably hurrying the second half of the line along a little, as if in excitement at rising on a summer morning. In a regular, conventional poem, we'd expect the second line to follow a similar pattern to the first. But, as a man and as an artist, Blake was far from regular or conventional. In his lifetime he was viewed at best as an eccentric, at worst as a madman and, certainly, Blake never liked to follow anyone else's rules. In the light of this, perhaps it's unsurprising that the second line immediately deviates from the pattern set by the first:

'When the **birds sing** on **every tree'**

This could be read as either a tetrameter or a pentameter, if we decide that the first word, 'when' should take a stress. Not only is there an uncertain stress pattern on the first two syllables of the line, but this is followed by two heavy stresses in succession – **birds sing** – which is called a spondee, before the line settles back into an iambic pattern at the end, though even then, a pendant might argue that 'every' can have three syllables, not two.

The poem's third line runs more smoothly along the groove of the iambic tetrameter:

'The **dis**tant **hunts**man **winds** his **horn'**

And this iambic metre is also maintained in the fourth line:

'And the **sky**-lark **sings** with **me'**

However, either this line is a stress short, as it's only a trimeter, with three beats, not the requisite four, or perhaps 'sky-lark' is another spondee, in which case the middle of the line would
have three strong beats bunched up in a row; **'sky-lark sings'.**

Deary me, it already seems that Mr. Blake just can't keep his metre under any kind of control. No sooner has he established a pattern that the poem slips out of it and goes its own way. At least, the full end-rhymes, arranged in a sonorous cross-rhymed structure, impose some sort of sonic order. But the balance and harmony these generate are undercut by Blake adding an extra, unexpected fifth line to his stanza, thereby unbalancing it with a third 'ee' rhyme, an effect exacerbated by more uncertain, wobbly metrics:

'O! what sweet company'

How would you scan that line? It could be:

'O! what **sweet com**pany'

That would make it another shorter line, a trimeter. Or perhaps the emotive first exclamative 'O' should be stressed to make a tetrameter, which would make the first two syllables trochaic, not iambic, or, indeed, anapaestic (two unstressed syllables followed by a stress). In any case, there's no clear iambic pattern and, via the rhyme scheme, the reader is forced to stress a syllable that wouldn't normally be stressed, the last letter of 'company', making what is called a 'wrenched line', normally an effect considered clumsy and amateurish in poetry. And all this is made even worse by Blake's decision to use the adjective 'sweet', as this only draws more sonic attention to the run of 'ee' rhymes, making us hear the last one as louder and more pronounced.

From the perspective of metrical orthodoxy, Blake's first stanza is so clumsily erratic and hopelessly irregular, so awkwardly out-of-kilter and seemingly ill-managed, that it's almost beyond repair.

In his primer on poetry, 'The Ode Less Travelled', Stephen Fry performs a similar metrical interrogation of some of Blake's verse and finds the lines from *Auguries of Innocence* 'messy, mongrel and mawkish'. Having mocked the 'scansion, syntax and manifold inconsistencies', Fry goes on to say, however, that such 'ill-made felicities' 'only go on to convince us of the work's fundamental honesty and authenticity'. Concluding his discussion with the famous quatrain beginning 'To see a world in a grain of sand', Fry writes that 'the metre is shot to hell in every line, but who cares. It is the real thing.'[2]

A child's voice

Perhaps, rather than being unintentionally uncultivated and unpolished, Blake's metrics are a bit rough around the edges and erratic because these qualities embody the voice of his speaker, a young, uncultivated schoolboy who loves the natural world but despises his harsh schooling. Perhaps the metrical looseness is essential to the sense of an authentic, natural, unpolished speaking voice. This speaking voice tells us a narrative that expresses Blake's world views, his sympathies and antipathies.

---

[2] Fry, 'The Ode Less Travelled', pp.70-73.

Although he was something of a singular one-off, Blake's work shares some characteristics with his fellow Romantic poets, such as Wordsworth and Coleridge, both of whom knew him a little. The veneration of childhood as a special state of existence and of nature as a spiritual sanctuary from the rapidly industrialising and urbanising world around him, for example, are key aspects of Romanticism. The emotive intensity of this poem, its capacity to move the heart as much as the brain, is another common characteristic, although the righteous rage at the injustices of the world is fiercer in Blake's poems, on the whole, than in the works of the other Romantics. In poem after poem, Blake raged against how his society abused human beings, and the worst of this abuse, for the poet, was the heartless exploitation of vulnerable children. Never is this exploitation more starkly depicted in his poems about chimney sweepers, in which a small child, sold into a brutal and miserably short life as a sweep is described merely as a 'little black thing in the snow'.

Great universal teachers

Coleridge called nature the 'great universal teacher', a striking contrast to how formal education is presented in *The School Boy*. The poem begins with feelings of love and, with the common Romantic symbol of a summer morning, suggesting new beginnings, fresh hope, energy and excitement, subtly underscored by the little metrical dexterity we have already noted. Ideas of liberty and joyful communion with nature are further established through the two references to birdsong. The birdsong seems ubiquitous - the 'birds sing on every tree' – and the boy too is singing, in harmony 'with' the 'skylark'. In English poetry, this little bird is especially associated with the dawn and with freedom and zest for life, because of the way it flies upward and out of sight while singing a merry, musical song that can last from dawn to well after sunrise. Often poets also find a religious significance to the sky-lark's flight, it's soaring up and up from muddy fields, like an angel ascending from earth to heaven. (See, for example, Shakespeare's description of his soul rising like a skylark from 'sullen ground' to 'sing hymns at heaven's gate' in Sonnet 29, fellow Romantic, Percy Bysshe Shelley's *To a Sky-Lark* and in music, Vaughan Wiliams' exquisite *The Lark Ascending*.) Perhaps for some readers, the figure of the huntsman might add a more ominous dimension, counterbalancing the joy of the first stanza, but his primary purpose is surely as another symbol of freedom.

The child is the father of the man

Sweetness, love, freedom, joy, vitality, companionship all these innocent, positive feelings are driven immediately away in the second and third stanzas. 'Sweet' 'love' is replaced by 'dismay'; 'freedom' by constraint and oppression 'under a cruel eye'; 'joy' by anxiety and dreariness; vitality by 'drooping' and being 'worn' out, and the child is alone as the weather turns, symbolically miserable, and it rains.

The fourth stanza expresses the heart of the poem's message, making explicit the link between birds and children. Joy and freedom, Blake opines, are natural birthrights, for both birds and boys, and caging both destroys their capacity to produce something joyous and beautiful, their natural songs. The initial, joyous exclamatory 'O' of the first stanza is echoed at the start of the penultimate stanza, but the change in tone emphasises the misery. It is the start of a plea to parents to embrace Blake's ideas on education. Not only will children caged in joyless forms of education not be able to sing, worse still, they will not develop the healthy vitality and robustness needed to thrive in later life. Blake switches to a second symbol, from his bird analogy to more imagery drawn from nature, 'tender' flowering plants. Making children suffer in schools will 'nip' their 'buds', blow away their 'blossoms' and strip them of joy. Returning back to the opening stanza, the symbolism then shifts again to the use of seasons in order to

emphasise the scale of the damage.

Children who are damaged as they grow up will not be able to express 'summer' 'joy' when they become adults, unable to produce 'summer fruits' nor will they be productive members of society. Clearly here, there is a sense of natural fertility being neutered, resulting in a bleak universal sterility. The damage is not, then, just to the individual children, but to society as a whole, which loses its expressions of summer and the benefits of summer fruits. If the latter are interpreted as symbolising the next generation of children, then the inability to produce fruit would signal a society set on course for terminal decline. If this isn't persuasive enough, Blake switches the seasons from summer to winter. At some points in life, he argues, we all will face difficult challenges, sorrows and griefs. Less resilient, less healthy children will become adults unable to recover, 'gather', from the destructive forces of grief. Nor will they have the wisdom to find meaning in aging. Nor will they be capable of withstanding the worst and most difficult things that life can throw at us, the 'blasts of winter'.

Notably the first four stanzas of *The School Boy* complete themselves in their final lines, ending with full-stops and a question mark. Not only is there a greater use of enjambment in the last two stanzas, but the penultimate stanza also runs on into the final one in a sentence stretching over seven lines. This culminates in a question mark after 'appear', but this is only really a brief pause, in a small intake of breath before the central argument continues in the following lines. The rhetorical momentum generated is aided by Blake's irregular and unconventional, but propulsive metrics. In the middle of the final stanza, instance, there's a quickening of the poem's pulse in successive lines, with 'or the **sum**mer **fruits** ap**pear**' and 'or how **shall** we **gath**er...' both beginning with anapaests. That said, as we indicated at the start of this essay, different readers may scan the lines differently, potentially stressing 'or', a significant word repeated three times at the start of successive lines. Or perhaps the 'how' is more important than the 'shall' – how will it be possible to recover from grief? Each reading of the metrics here is valid, but, however these lines are scanned, what is undoubted is the passionate intensity of Blake's message.

The Schoolboy crunched:

SUMMER – BIRDS – HUNTSMAN – SINGS – COMPANY – SCHOOL – DRIVES – CRUEL – LITTLE – DISMAY – DROOPING – ANXIOUS – DELIGHT – BOWER – SHOWER – BORN – CAGE – FEARS – WING – SPRING – NIPP'D – BLOSSOMS – STRIPP'D – JOY – SORROW – HOW – FRUITS – GATHER – BLASTS

William Wordsworth, *I Wandered Lonely as a Cloud*

A Romantic lyric poem, *I Wandered Lonely as a Cloud* (1807) is perhaps the best known of William Wordsworth's work. Also commonly referred to simply as *Daffodils*, this lyric poem conveys the beauty of nature and its inspirational and restorative powers. This poem is amongst the most famous poems from the Romantic era, and epitomises Wordsworth's own view, as expressed in the preface to his 'Lyrical Ballads': 'Poetry is the spontaneous overflow of powerful feelings: it takes its origin from emotion recollected in tranquillity'. As one of the most well-known poems in the English language, it has been subject to multiple parodies – the rock band Genesis in their 1974 song *The Colony of Slippermen* is just one example – but remains emblematic of Romanticism and the transformative and therapeutic effects of the natural world.

We wandered lonely as two clouds

On 15th April 1802, Wordsworth went on a walk with his sister Dorothy in the Lake District. It was the experience of this walk, and reading his sister's subsequent journal entry about it, that moved the poet to write *I Wandered Lonely as a Cloud*. 'I never saw daffodils so beautiful,' Dorothy wrote in her journal, 'they grew among the mossy stones about and above them; some rested their heads upon these stones, as on a pillow, for weariness; and the rest tossed and reeled and danced'. This sentiment is echoed in the poem's opening stanza, as the speaker sees a 'host of golden daffodils... Fluttering and dancing in the breeze'. That same personification, 'danced', used in both Dorothy's diary entry and throughout the poem, conveys the joy evoked by the sudden, unexpected sight of the daffodils. The use of present participle verbs, 'fluttering' and 'dancing', suggests that the delight that the speaker experienced continues long after the walk came to an end and, hence, the ongoing benefits of being immersed in natural landscapes.

I Wandered Lonely as a Cloud is written in iambic tetrameter, a rhythm that mirrors the 'fluttering' and 'dancing' of the daffodils themselves, as well as the energy that the speaker felt upon seeing them. Nature continues to 'dance' through every stanza, a repetition that suggests continuity in the joy and inspiration sparked by the sight of the flowers. What we would now call the mental health benefits of being immersed in natural landscapes, this extended personification suggests, are profound and long-lasting. Asserting the enduring value of the natural world was particularly important to Wordsworth and to other Romantics, because nature was coming increasingly under threat in a society that was rapidly industrialising. Although his readership may have been largely metropolitan, throughout his poetry, Wordsworth celebrated and championed the countryside.

Significantly, the opening of the poem does not describe the daffodils themselves, however, but the speaker's own apparent solitude. He 'wandered lonely as a cloud', a famous opening line that conveys feelings of isolation and detachment. Interestingly deleting Dorothy's presence from the poem, the simile suggests that inspiration comes to the isolated, but also receptive individual. Wordsworth doesn't have to set off to find inspiration or doggedly to track it down, rather, he drifts like a cloud, without any clear sense of direction. To wander means the freedom to go where you will, untethered by obligations or plans. Indeed 'wandering' is the archetypal means of locomotion for Romantic poets – see, for example, William Blake's London or W. B. Yeats' The Song of Wandering Aengus. While the verb suggests freedom, it also contains the potential to lose oneself. In Wordsworth's case, it seems to have resulted rather in the loss of any acknowledgement of his sister's contribution to his most famous poem.

Wordsworth's comparison of himself to the natural world highlights the connection between man and nature, even before he sees the daffodils, suggestive of the intense bond between humanity and nature. The daffodils are described as 'a crowd/A host' in this opening stanza. The multiple collective nouns could be viewed as tautologous, perhaps conveying the speaker's overwhelming delight and the challenge of expressing his overflow of emotions in words. However, the two words have slightly different meanings. Whilst the 'crowd' suggests how abundant the daffodils were, the 'host' has a welcoming quality, as if the flowers have invited the speaker into a new way of being and seeing the world. These almost hyperbolic descriptions convey the Romantic belief in nature's spiritually uplifting and restorative powers.

The poem's second and third stanzas continue to focus on the daffodils in detail. They are as 'Continuous as the stars that shine/ And twinkle on the milky way', a simile that emphasises the daffodils' abundance as well as their ability to brighten the speaker's mood. Throughout the Romantic era, there was a fascination with the sublime (a feeling of awe and even terror stirred usually by nature or art). Stars can be seen as a symbol of the sublime and through the comparison of the daffodils to stars, Wordsworth suggests the 'never-ending' endurance of the natural world. Significantly, the daffodils are lined on 'the margin of a bay'. Whilst this is in part a literal description, providing a vivid image of their presence, it is also, arguably, a metaphor. This imagery of liminality, the threshold between one place and another where earth and water meet, highlights the way in which this encounter with the natural world transports the speaker into a spiritual realm, beyond his earthly solitude and into a deeper contemplative state.

A vacant or pensive mood

The third stanza spills into the fourth, a continuation that structurally encapsulates one of the poem's key themes: the power of memory to retain and even transform experience into something profound. The speaker 'gazed and gazed' on the daffodils, but it is not until later that he realises their 'wealth'. The beauty of the daffodils has an instantaneous effect on the speaker, emphasised by the repetition of 'gazed', a line that further captures the key Romantic belief in the power of nature to soothe, captivate and inspire. This Romantic notion is reinforced by the metaphorical 'wealth' that the daffodils provide; they are emotionally enriching not only in the present but later, in the speaker's memory of the experience.

The act of remembering the daffodils, once the speaker is at home on his 'couch', troubled by thoughts or by the lack of them, is the subject of the final stanza. The daffodils 'flash upon that inward eye… And then my heart with pleasure fills'. The poet suggests that natural beauty, such as the sight of the daffodils, has a transformative and restorative effect on human emotions, but that we only come to appreciate how profound this effect can be afterwards, through the act of remembering. The rhyme of 'fills' and 'daffodils' to end the poem neatly encapsulates Romantic veneration of the natural world and the power of nature to provoke deep emotional understanding, as it is immersion in nature that truly relieves solitude, sparks the imagination and provides joy and comfort. Juxtaposing of 'bliss' and 'solitude' is further suggestive of the happiness that can be found in contemplation of nature's beauty; being alone is not synonymous with loneliness, particularly when the mind is filled with memories as nature's beauty.

In memory
Doubleness, or twoness, is encoded into the structure of Wordsworth's poem. The opening four lines of each of the four stanzas have a cross-rhyme pattern, with two full rhymes at the ends. There are also two rhyme patterns in operation: each stanza concludes with a couplet. Drawing two lines together, these couplets also end with a further two full rhymes. Generating a sense of musical harmony, the significance of this structural feature seems obvious in a poem about man and nature. There is, however, also a less pronounced, tripartite pattern - the three rhyme sounds in each stanza, such as 'cloud', 'hills' and 'trees' in the first stanza. In a poem where the first-person pronoun is used emphatically and repeatedly, 'I wandered', 'I saw' etc. is it too fanciful to suggest we can read this subtle threeness as symbolically or subconsciously including another figure in the poem, Wordsworth's sister, Dorothy?

I Wandered Lonely as a Cloud crunched:

WANDERED – FLOATS – I – HOST – LAKE – DANCING – STARS – TWINKLE – NEVER-ENDING – MARGIN – GLANCE – HEADS – DANCED – GLEE – POET – COMPANY – GAZED – WEALTH – OFT – PENSIVE – INWARD – SOLITUDE – HEART - DAFFODILS

Elizabeth Barrett Browning, Sonnet 29, I think of thee!

A modest disguise

Elizabeth Barrett Browning's Sonnet 29, I think of thee, is a poem of intense and passionate yearning for an absent lover. If you've been in love and experienced how you can't seem to stop thinking about that person when they are not with you, so that your thoughts seem out-of-control and threaten to overwhelm you, then you will recognise what the poet expresses in this poem. She wrote it as a private expression of her love for the poet Robert Browning, with whom she had begun a secret courtship. The couple later married, but her father disowned her as he did not approve of her choice. It was only after they were married that Elizabeth mentioned she had written a series of sonnets about her husband while they were courting. When he read them, he was convinced they were the best sonnets written in English since Shakespeare's and encouraged her to publish. However, they were so personal and revealing, having never been intended for anyone other than Elizabeth Barrett Browning herself, that they were published under the title Sonnets from the Portuguese, in an attempt to pretend they were obscure translations of another poet, rather than intimate expressions of her own private emotions. This accounts for the intensely personal tone of *Sonnet 29*; when we write about this poem, we can confidently talk about the poet's own feelings rather than those of a dramatized speaker, although inevitably there is always some act of dramatization to any poem, regardless of how closely and accurately the poet wants to express their own personality in their work.

A technical challenge

To fully appreciate Barrett Browning's art and achievement in this poem, we first need to understand something of the poetic form in which she chose to compose it - the sonnet. In the twentieth and twenty-first centuries, poets have experimented greatly with sonnets, but traditionally they tend to be love poems and have a very strict poetic structure that places a number of rules or limitations on the poet, making sonnets a challenge to write. Sonnets must have fourteen lines and tend to be written in iambic pentameter, lines of ten syllables that alternate between an unstressed and a stressed syllable, as in the opening line of *Sonnet 29* where Barrett Browning writes 'I **think** of **thee**! - my **thoughts** do **twine** and **bud**'. Sonnets also tend to follow a distinctive rhyming pattern. There are different variations of sonnets depending on how the ideas are arranged and what the rhyme scheme is, but the most common types are the Petrarchan (also known as Italian) sonnet, the Spenserian and the Shakespearean sonnet. *Sonnet 29* is written as a Petrarchan sonnet, probably the most challenging form for writers in English due to the more limited number of rhymes. Traditionally Petrarchan sonnets are divided into an octave of eight lines (rhyming abbaabba) that presents a problem, followed by a sestet of six lines, which presents the solution. The rhyme scheme for the sestet can be more flexible but tends to follow cdecde or cdcdcd. The transition from the octave to the sestet where the poem shifts from a problem to a solution occurs between the eighth and ninth lines and is known as a *volta*, which means 'turn' in Italian. Barret Browning was an accomplished sonnet writer and most of her sonnets follow the rules impeccably, but what makes this poem remarkable is the way in which she deliberately breaks some of the rules of the sonnet to create particular effects and communicate specific meanings that powerfully reveal the intense emotions she was feeling.

An example of this rule-breaking is immediately obvious in Barret

Browning's poetic form, where she entwines the octave and sestet through her rhyme scheme, abbaabba cbcbcb, with the b rhyme from the octave weaving its way into the sestet. In fact, it's even more complex than that due to the poem's sentence structures as the sestet actually comprises two tercets, one rhymed cbc, then another rhymed bcb. This means she has chosen an envelope rhyme, a rhyme scheme that creates backward momentum and circularity, where the rhyme sounds 'insphere' each other, delivering a sonic entanglement that chimes perfectly with the encircling 'wild vines' Barret Browning describes suffocating the symbolic 'strong tree of the poem.

My thoughts do twine and bud

Although the poem was originally only intended for Elizabeth herself, she starts by addressing her future husband, Robert Browning, when she writes 'I think of thee!' The exclamation mark emphasises the excitement he makes her feel, as do the short, simple, monosyllabic words that create the impression that nothing else is important to her. The archaic pronoun 'thee' also generates a much more intimate tone than using 'you' might and appears seven times in the poem, demonstrating just how important and all-encompassing her future husband was to her. 'Thee' also suggests, particularly as Barrett Browning was a devout Christian, the religious language of the King James Bible, where it appears 2,738 times, elevating her love for Robert Browning almost into the spiritual sphere of devotional love for God.

However, no sooner does the poet begin to think of her love than her thoughts are interrupted by the dash in line one, which creates a pause in the rhythm, known as a caesura. The caesura again emphasises the importance of 'thee' by forcing us to dwell on this word, but it also suggests the poet is not quite in control of her thoughts, as if they are taking on a life and direction of their own. This leads into the next part of the poem where Barrett Browning introduces the poem's central image:

'my thoughts do twine and bud/ About thee, as wild vines, about a tree'. Here, she uses a simile to compare her thoughts about Robert to a vine that wraps itself around the trunk of a tree as it climbs up and smothers the tree's bark. She draws once again on Biblical language, this time from *Song of Songs* in *The Old Testament*, where the female speaker in the book also compares her love to a palm tree and says 'thy stature is like to a palm tree…I will take hold of the boughs thereof: now also thy breasts shall be as clusters of the vine'. *Song of Songs* is a celebration of sexual love and there is an equally charged, erotic dimension to Barrett Browning's poem, the verb 'twine' suggestive of the poet wrapping herself around her lover, the adjective 'wild' evocative of an uncontrolled release of passion and desire, and the image of the tree a barely disguised phallic symbol. Such details might make a prudish reader blush even today; imagine, then, how shocking the poem's sentiments might have been to the average Victorian reader, particularly so as the writer of this sensual, erotic material is, of course, a lady.

However, while she delights in her love, the problem for the poet is that her thoughts and emotions seem to be growing out-of-control, something she cleverly evokes through enjambment. Her thoughts in line one, for example, spill over into line two. The caesuras after 'thee' and 'vines' in line two also suggest the sudden growth of ideas or a change of direction, as if her thoughts are wrapping themselves around the poem like the vines around the tree. Irrepressible growth is also evoked through the way the simile comparing her thoughts to a vine and the man she loves to a tree evolves into an extended metaphor - also known as a conceit - that weaves itself throughout the whole poem. The central problem that the octave presents is that the poet's overpowering thoughts for this man are clouding and obscuring the man himself, so that she can no longer see him clearly. He becomes more and more submerged under her thoughts, in the same way a vine might grow up and around a tree, hiding its bark and true form. As she says in the next two lines, 'and soon there's nought to see/ Except the straggling green which hides the wood'. Here, the verb 'straggling' gives a strong sense of the way her thoughts have become unkempt and overgrown. We can also almost hear the word 'strangling', which is what a vine eventually does to a tree if left unchecked, implying that her thoughts risk completing destroying the true image of the man himself. But as she determines in line six, 'I will not have my thoughts instead of thee'. For the solution to her problem, we now need to turn to the sonnet's sestet.

Rustle thy boughs

In a traditional Petrarchan sonnet, the volta, which indicates the turn of thought towards a solution, normally happens between the eighth and ninth lines. In *Sonnet 29*, however, it occurs earlier in lines 7-8 where the poet pleads with her love to 'Rather, instantly/ Renew thy presence'. The simple solution to the poet's problem of her out-of-control longing for her love is for him to appear and no longer be absent. Barrett Browning deliberately places the volta earlier than it should be in a sonnet to express her impatience to see her love, the overwhelming love she feels for him causing her to throw aside the normal rules and strictures of traditional sonnet writing. This sense of urgency and excitement is also captured in the enjambment at the end of the seventh line, which hastens the reader onto the next line without time for pause or hesitation. Her insistence that he comes to her immediately to bridge their absence is further accentuated through imperative verbs throughout this section, such as the command in line nine to 'Rustle thy boughs and set thy trunk all bare'. She also reverses the rhythm of the poem at the start of this line by using a trochee (a stressed syllable followed by an unstressed, as in '**Rust**le') rather than an iamb (an unstressed syllable followed by a stressed, as in 'Re**new**' in the previous line). This reversal emphasises the force of the poet's command to her love but also the reversal of her thoughts overpowering the image of her love. By appearing to her and revealing his true self, rather than the distorted version her thoughts have created, she commands the virile tree to shake free of the vine that has enshrouded and cloaked it.

In fact, the sestet is markedly different to the octave in its scansion. Whereas the octave is mostly perfectly iambic pentameter verse, the sestet is notably less controlled; Barret Browning adds extra syllables and at times an extra beat, making some lines hypermetrical, giving them a sonic intensity proportional to the potent fantasy energising the end of the poem. This is most acute in the line, 'Drop <u>heav</u> i ly <u>down</u> - <u>burst</u>, <u>shatt</u> ered, <u>eve</u> ry <u>where</u>' which represents the poem's climactic release.

Barrett Browning also uses sibilance to great effect in this section. Examples include lines eight and nine, in which words such as 'presence', 'as', 'strong', 'should', 'Rustle', 'boughs' and 'set', evoke the sound of rustling leaves as the tree breaks free of the vines. Enjambment is again used to striking effect, as when she commands her love to 'let these bands of greenery which insphere thee/ Drop heavily down', forcing the reader to drop down the lines as the vine leaves fall from the tree. The alliteration of the plosive 'd' sounds in 'Drop heavily down' further emphasises the forcefulness with which the tree shakes itself free, as does the violence of the verbs 'burst' and 'shattered' later in the line. The caesura in the middle of this line after 'down' creates a momentary pause, long enough to build up the energy that reaches a triumphant climax of 'burst, shattered, everywhere!', which reaches its crescendo by building up a one, two and then three syllable word, followed by the emphatic exclamation.

This deep joy

The poem's final sentence which runs across the last three lines envisages an end to the lovers' separation. The anticipation the poet feels and 'the deep joy to see and hear thee', as she imagines her love's presence, is captured in the simple, monosyllabic words, the line's extra eleventh syllable, as well as the enjambment that flows seamlessly onto the penultimate line. Now that her thoughts no longer obscure her love from view, she can see him clearly and 'breathe within thy shadow a new air' in language that again echoes the female lover of Song of Songs who says of her love, 'I sat down under his shadow with great delight, and his fruit was sweet to my taste'. The poem's final line enacts a full reversal of the poem's opening; where the poet began by acknowledging 'I think of thee', now she reveals 'I do not think of thee'. This is not because he has become unimportant to her - far from it! Rather now, in his imagined presence, the poet states 'I am too near to thee'. Her thoughts about her love have now been replaced by something far better - the man himself. This is the seventh time the word 'thee' occurs in the poem, a number which in the Bible symbolizes completeness and perfection. The poet also draws attention to this word by making it the eleventh syllable of a line we would expect to end after ten, while also breaking the rhyming pattern of the sestet by using repetition of 'thee' at the end of lines ten, twelve and fourteen rather than rhymed words. Barrett Browning seems to be deliberately breaking the rules of the sonnet writing to suggest that perfection is not to be found in poetry, but rather in her lover, and not even the age-old rules and structures of that most traditional of love poems - the sonnet -can contain and constrain her powerful and joyful love for him.

Sonnet 29 crunched:

THEE – VINES – NOUGHT – STRAGGLING – O – INSTEAD – DEARER – TREE – BARE – BANDS – SHATTERED – JOY – BREATHE – NEAR

Christina Rossetti, *Cousin Kate*

Sit in gold and sing

Probably most teachers and pupils have had the experience of slogging through endless close textual analysis of an anthology of poetry, especially in the run up to examinations. It's important, I think, for teachers to try to leaven this brain-centred, analytical diet with more creative, aesthetic and emotional approaches to poetry. Composed in a ballad metre, Rossetti's tragic dramatic monologue could certainly be approached through creative writing. It seems likely that pupils engaging with the poem in this way are more likely to become interested in both the developments of its narrative and in the technical challenges, such as the skill required to deliver double quatrains in which every even line rhymes.

Perhaps give the class the first two stanzas with line 14 blanked out. Set them to try to identify if there is a regular metre and if so, what this is, and the rhyme scheme. From this they should be able to arrive at the 'glove' rhyme or generate their own alternative. Now give them the third stanza which introduces a new character into this story of exploitation, gender, power and class. Again, blank out one line, line 20, and give them a couple of teacher minutes to see if they can work it out. Do the same with stanza four, this time blanking out the particularly hard-hitting line, number 28. This apprentice work should set them up for the challenge of constructing a final stanza and a satisfying end to the story. I'd be inclined to just give them the first word of this stanza 'yet' as that signals a new turn of events, some new and significant factor in the story. After ten teacher minutes see what they've come up with and discuss. When they're ready, reveal the first half of the last stanza, up to the word 'fret'. A couple of minutes in pairs should be enough for them to try to work out what this 'gift' might be and why it might make Kate worry so.

The ruined maid

Writer of the hymn *In the Bleak Midwinter*, Christina Rossetti [1830-1894] was one of the foremost Victorian poets. Born into a highly talented, Anglo-Italian artistic family, her poetic ability was obvious from an early age; she had, for instance, poems accepted for publication when she was just seventeen years old. Her brother, Dante Gabriel Rossetti was the poet and painter who established the 'Pre-Raphaelite' brotherhood with its distinctive dreamy medieval aesthetic. Her father was a celebrated scholar of Dante.

Rossetti championed progressive causes and particularly the rights of women, not only in her art, but also in her life. She volunteered, for example, to join Florence Nightingale's nurses during the Crimean War, and later volunteered at a charitable institution for the reclamation of 'fallen women' working with women who had children out of wedlock and with prostitutes. Rossetti's concern for women sexually exploited by more powerful men and then scorned by polite society, is, of course, reflected in *Cousin Kate*.

The narrator of Rossetti's poem is an ordinary country girl. She describes herself as a type, a lowly, virginal 'cottage-maiden', who was 'contented' with her lot in life until her beauty is discovered by a 'great lord'. Even at this earliest stage of the poem, Rossetti makes us aware that this will be no romantic tale of love overcoming the barriers of class. The repeated 'why' questions and the last line of the first stanza make clear the downwards direction the narrative must travel. And, it's a familiar, almost archetypal, narrative of a poor girl flattered into a relationship with a much richer, more powerful, higher status man, a lord. The verb 'lured' suggests that the lord deliberately manipulates the girl, tempting her to join him in his more luxurious life. Later she refers to being 'bought' by his 'land'. She is only a humble 'cottage-maiden', whereas he lives in a grand 'palace-home'. The contrast could not be starker and the rags-to-riches temptation understandable. Her corruption swiftly follows and soon she is living a 'shameless shameful life', presumably as the lord's mistress. It's an interesting contradictory phrase and suggests the speaker's deep ambivalence, or perhaps the difference between how others perceived her and how she perceives herself. Clearly, she feels degraded, reduced to a mere decorative object for the lord's vanity, as the similes comparing her to a 'golden knot' and to a 'glove' evince. Knots, of course, can be constricting and gloves can easily be removed. Poignantly the young woman describes herself as an 'unclean thing'. Dehumanising herself, using the language of purity and dirtiness, she applies Victorian societal values to condemn her ruined state. The situation is made more tragic by her awareness of how life could easily have been so different - she could have been pure and free, like a 'dove'.

So ends the first episode of the story. The young woman has become a 'plaything' for her lord's idle entertainment and the 'love' he gives her is of a very debased sort. Using this word, 'love' in this context, only highlights the lack of true love. A better, more accurate, truer word, would be 'lust'. Victorian patriarchal values meant that while a woman who had a sexual relationship out of wedlock was 'ruined' or 'fallen', and thought of as being akin to a prostitute, her male partner escaped censure almost entirely. This sexual and gender-based hypocrisy is the central subject of Thomas Hardy's devastating novel, 'Tess of the D'Urbervilles' written a few decades after Rossetti's poem. Certainly, the 'great lord' does not appear to have been affected by his affair or by having a mistress. At worst, scandal might have prevented him from marrying, especially from marrying another country girl.

Starkly, the following three stanzas contrast the rise of Cousin Kate with the fall of the narrator. When the lord turns his attention to her cousin, the narrator is dropped like a stone. However, Cousin Kate does not give in to sexual temptation, remaining 'so good and pure' she is the virtuous opposite of an 'unclean thing'. Consequently, the lord marries her. In contrast, the narrator repeats the description of herself as an inhuman object, only this time the focus is on her rejection by society, the same neighbours who have praised her cousin label her an 'outcast thing'. Rossetti underlines the moralising point she is making by repeating the information that the cousin was 'good and pure'. Consequently, Kate reaps the benefits - sitting in 'gold' to 'sing', while, in juxtaposition, the speaker can only 'howl' like a crazed animal, in 'dust'. Not only does the speaker suffer others' scorn, she thinks of herself as corrupted and seems to loathe herself for her own actions.

Cling closer

It is no consolation that if the order had been different, if the lord had seen Kate first, the speaker might have escaped her ruination. But she can console herself that despite the condemnation of the world, she would not have behaved in the same way as her cousin did, taking this exploiting lord for her husband when she did not love him. Hence the narrator casts doubt over Kate's supposed moral superiority.

The final stanza introduces the twist in the tale and the speaker's true consolation. It's implied that Kate and her lord will struggle to conceive as the narrator says she has the 'gift' of a child, whereas this is not something they seem 'like to get'. Once again Rossetti uses paradoxical language to express the speaker's ambivalent feelings - she refers to her son as 'my shame, my pride'. There is spirit and defiance and tenderness here that will keep the young woman going. In a surprising final turn of the story, it to this child the last four lines are addressed, eclipsing Kate in the speaker's attentions. Why does she tell him to 'cling closer, closer yet'? Is this tenderness and because she wants to protect him? Or is Rossetti a bit harder and less sentimental? Isn't there something perhaps a little calculating, an awareness maybe that her son is valuable in other ways? After all, she knows the lord 'would give broads lands' for a son to wear his 'coronet'.

From our perspective, it may seem that the villain of Rossetti's poem is the exploitative great lord, abusing his power and position to take advantage of and 'ruining' pretty peasant girls or, at a pinch, the hypocritical societal values that labelled women 'fallen' and 'ruined' and made them outcasts, while not condemning the men who exploited them. From the perspective of the narrator, however, it seems that Cousin Kate might be as much to blame and as much the object of her ire. Rather than support and sisterhood, the poem presents us with a bitter rivalry between its two female leads. This rivalry, as much as the lord, is the source of the conflict in Rossetti's poem.

Cousin Kate crushed:

COTTAGE-MAIDEN - HARDENED - CONTENTED - FAIR - WHY - PRAISE - LORD - CARE - LURED - WOE'S - SHAMEFUL - PLAYTHING - KNOT - GLOVE - UNCLEAN - DOVE - O - MORE - SAW - CAST - WATCHED - SPORT - MEAN - HIGH - PURE - RING - NEIGHBOURS - OUTCAST - HOWL - GOLD - TENDERER - STRONGER - TRUE - SAND - IF - IF - WON - BOUGHT - SPIT - HAND - YET - NOT - ALL - FRET - PRIDE - CLOSER - LANDS – CORONET

Thomas Hardy, *Drummer Hodge*

Drummer Hodge by Victorian novelist and poet Thomas Hardy describes the tragic death of a young, anonymous soldier during the Second Boer War (1899-1902). In emotionally restrained, dignified verse, Hardy depicts Drummer Hodge's rushed burial in a barren wasteland in South Africa, far, far away from the comforts of home. What Hardy leaves out of this short narrative poem is as important as what he includes: firstly, there's no exciting dramatization of battle itself, unlike in poems such as Tennyson's exhilarating *Charge of the Light Brigade*, written half a century earlier; secondly, by giving the reader no explanation of how or why this lad has died or what for, Hardy makes this death seem a futile waste of a young life; and, lastly, the lack of care or grief or mourning after his death and the way his body is disposed of, like a piece of rubbish, powerfully conveys the common, casual brutalities of war; Thus the poet uses his elegy to critique war and its dehumanising, destructive effects.

Uncoffined

From the poem's opening stanza, Hardy presents the cruel and senseless nature of war. The body of Drummer Hodge is 'Uncoffined', a word created by Hardy and emphatically placed at the start of the line to highlight the lack of time and resources available for a proper, respectful burial. The use of off-hand, dismissive language, such as 'throw in' and 'just as found', conveys how rushed the burial was and how lacking in sentiment. There was no time for a ceremony or any proper period of grieving. In addition, unfamiliar terms, such as 'kopje-crest', meaning a small hill, 'veldt', a reference to the open land of southern Africa, and

'Karoo', a barren plain, are drip-fed through the poem. Such unfamiliar words emphasise the unfamiliarity of the surroundings and highlight just how far this young lad has strayed from his homeland in rural England. When the poem was published in his collection *Poems of the Past and Present* in 1901, Hardy changed the title, which had initially been *The Dead Drummer*. Whilst this original title captures the deindividualising nature of war, Hardy's revised title humanises Drummer Hodge, reminding us that every soldier who lost their lives in such wars deserves to be remembered. Although, as we shall see, the name 'Hodge' had a specific contemporary significance, its repetition in each stanza, ensures at least that he is remembered, while also drawing attention to how many individual identities are lost and forgotten in warfare.

The choice of the 'Drummer' serves as a reminder of just how young this victim of war would have been; military drummers, who played music as the battles began, were often too young to fight as regular soldiers. Probably this drummer would not have been much more than a boy. Contemporarily, 'Hodge' was a common name for a country dweller or a farm labourer. A derogatory term, it would have been given as a nickname to someone considered to be unsophisticated and from the country - so this isn't actually the dead boy's real name. Sadly, even in death, he isn't granted the dignity of having his real name and identity restored, carrying, instead the pejorative and generalised term 'Hodge' with him into his grave. Clearly, he is an everyman figure, standing in for all the numberless other ordinary and often anonymous victims of wars.

In novels such as 'Tess of the D'Urbervilles', 'Jude the Obscure', among others, as well as in his poetry, Hardy often wrote about the lives of working-class individuals, often presenting his working-class characters sympathetically and using his writing to criticise class inequalities and prejudices. The choice of 'Hodge' may also convey the dismissive attitude of a powerful Victorian elite, who viewed common soldiers as dispensable, merely pawns in a bigger political picture.

In contrast to the named Drummer Hodge, the poem opens with the impersonal pronoun 'They', the soldiers who lay Hodge to rest. This emphasises how far this drummer was from his loved ones when he died, as he is buried by faceless, nameless individuals. It also reinforces how such tragedies would be a common occurrence: without apparent care or feeling, they simply 'throw' his body into an unmarked grave. Opening with this nameless plural pronoun epitomises one of the poem's key themes: the deindividualizing, brutalising impact of warfare.

Foreign constellations

The first stanza ends with the imagery of the stars, the 'foreign constellations west', which draws attention to the theme of fate. The description of the stars as 'foreign', combined with the repeated adjective 'strange', convey how unfamiliar these skies were to him, capturing the alienating experience of journeying abroad to serve in the army. Stars, furthermore, are traditionally symbols of fate. There is a pattern of celestial imagery at the end of each stanza, with 'Strange stars amid the gloom... strange-eyed constellations reign/ His stars eternally' in the second and third stanzas respectively. The 'Strange' constellations may portray the meaninglessness of his death and perhaps the nonsensical nature of war itself, leading to so many innocent lives being lost. The use of sibilance, such as 'southern trees' and 'strange stars', creates a subtly sinister tone, highlighting the harsh reality of war and creating a haunting mood, a reminder of the lives lost during the war. It mirrors the stillness of the natural world, which continues on long after lives – such as Drummer

Hodge's – have been cut short all too soon. Whereas the constellations are 'foreign' in the first stanza, they are 'strange-eyed' in the third and final stanza. The eternal presence of the stars, combined with the personification 'strange-eyed', contrast poignantly with the drummer boy's short life, suggesting the inevitability of fate and the transience of individual human lives compared to the permanence of nature. Considering an alternative interpretation, there is something poetic about the celestial imagery. The stars, by the final line, are 'His stars eternally'. The personal pronoun suggests a duality to his fate, both isolation and belonging, as if his tragic destiny were inevitable as soon as his identity became that of a drummer. There is perhaps too some consolation in the idea that in some ways he endures as part of the landscape, his 'breast and brain/ Grown to some Southern tree'.

The celestial imagery contrasts with descriptions of the drummer boy's home, reminding readers of the cruel and destructive nature of war. He is miles and miles from his 'Wessex home', and his 'homely Northern breast and brain' contrasts with the eternal stars. The repetition of 'home' and 'homely' underscores how unfamiliar these South African surroundings would have been for him. Wessex is an imaginary county in south-west England, a location that Hardy uses throughout his fiction to explore recurring themes such as rural life and class status. The use of 'Wessex' as Drummer Hodge's homeland accentuates the contrast between the rural land that he is familiar with and the 'foreign' land where he dies. This juxtaposition between Wessex and South Africa illustrates the dislocating, alienating nature of his death and the unforgiving nature of war.

Hardy's poem critiques the patriotism and imperialism that dominated Victorian Britain and underpinned the motivations behind the Boer War, by demonstrating a critical attitude towards romantic glorifications of war, which led to too many young lives being too easily and quickly sacrificed. There are shifts in time between the stanzas. The first stanza is in the present tense, focusing on what has happened to Hodge, emphasising the brutal and ruthless nature of war. The second stanza shifts to the past tense, reflecting on the drummer boy's life and how little he understood about the circumstances that led him to be in South Africa and fighting in the Boer War. The third stanza is in the future tense, centring on his burial place and how nature will continue to grow as he becomes one with the environment. There is also a sense of contrast in this poignant ending, between the natural world, which continues to 'reign', and his own short existence and seemingly meaningless death.

Hardy's poem, then, is a moving reflection on the devastating impacts of war. Through the depiction of Drummer Hodge, the poet draws attention to the lives of ordinary, too-often forgotten individuals and the way in which they can, tragically, be seen as expendable.

A memorial in verse

Notably, Hardy's poem is written in a very regular, formal pattern, with three six-line stanzas following a consistent alternating rhyme scheme (ABABAB), with full, masculine rhymes. Each line is also underpinned by a regular ballad metre, i.e. alternating lines of four beats and three beats, tetrameters and trimeters. What is the effect of this choice of form? Allied to the understated, sombre tone, perhaps the great care that has gone into this elegant, formal arrangement should be read as a kind of tribute, an attempt by the poet to restore some of the dignity and respect to this young victim of war through elegiac verse. In lieu of the dignity and respect the drummer boy was not given either in his short life or his death, but, like all human beings, he should have been given and deserved, in this poem Hardy remembers, mourns for and honours him.

Drummer Hodge crunched:

THROW – UNCOFFINED – LANDMARK – VELDT – FOREIGN – MOUND – YOUNG – WESSEX – MEANING – BUSH – WHY – STRANGE – YET – EVER – HOMELY – GROW – REIGN – ETERNALLY

Claude McKay, *I Shall Return*

Claude McKay, Jamaican by origin, was a notable figure in the evolving Harlem Renaissance of the 1920s and 1930s, an American cultural movement celebrating black art in all its forms, whether literary, artistic, musical or intellectual. This poem, from his 1922 collection 'Harlem Shadows', looks back towards Jamaica, to remember, celebrate and possibly, idealise, his homeland.

Nostalgic simplicity or simplistic nostalgia?

This sweet Shakespearian sonnet is saturated in nostalgia for simpler times and simpler lives, and like most nostalgia it could be over-simplifying that reality. McKay had already celebrated simpler, purer peasant lives in an earlier collection, 'Songs of Jamaica' (1912), written while in Jamaica, but here he does it from a substantial spatial distance, from the bracingly different urban hub of Harlem. Harlem's exciting cultural energies and modernist adventurism seems a long way from the rural utopia portrayed in this poem. Certainly the choice of the Shakespearean sonnet is fitting for McKay's rapturous recreation of his Jamaican heritage as well as his passionate articulation of his deep love for it.

It is undoubtedly a loving portrait of the 'native life' of his island where the landscape is an awe-inspiring paradise and the culture engendered there seems wholesomely and deeply rooted in the land itself. No wonder that the speaker is so intent to 'return again'. The lush tropical landscape is rendered in visual imagery of high value: The 'golden noon' and 'sapphire skies' both resonate with connotations of precious metals and jewels, the island bedecked in natural decoration. Not only is it visually beautiful, it's the anticipated effect of the speaker too that is notable: to return to the physical homeland is to return to a place that inspires him 'to laugh and love and watch with wonder eyes'. The gorgeous euphony of the alliterative Ls and Ws here is striking with their smooth, gentle music. That said, the visual of the 'forest fires' introduces a note of danger perhaps, or even destruction, and it doesn't sit comfortably with the previous glowing visuals. Notably the sound patterns become less pleasant too, with the more aggressive Fs of 'forest fires' and the Bs of 'burn...blue-black' working with the spiky fricatives of 'blue-black smoke to sapphire skies' to undermine the supposed utopia being described. Is this deliberate though? The sonic effect seems to undermine rather than underscore the intended impression of awesome, natural beauty. It is almost as if human activity is a danger to nature, at odds, rather than in harmony, with nature. So, could it be either a complex portrait of Jamaica or an example of where poetic intention is not realised fully, description and sound effects pulling in different directions?

Regardless, the second quatrain switches focus from the beautiful colours of the landscape to the life-giving water flowing through it. McKay captures the contrasting slowness *and* swiftness of the island's natural water systems. The slower pace of island life is associated with its streams, conveyed effectively in his choice of the easy-going verb 'loiter'. These leisurely waterways bring nourishment and fertility to the potentially parched tropical landscape: they 'bathe the brown blades of the bending grasses'. The 'bending,' lilting grasses and the streams work in harmony with each other. But what exactly does he mean when he wants to 'realize once more my thousand dreams' of torrents of water rushing down the mountain passes? Does he mean that rushing waterfalls in the mountains of Jamaica are but a dream *or* that he had dreamed of real Jamaican waterfalls a thousand times in his time away from home? It's not exactly clear.

Nevertheless, the general gist is positive and overall it does suggest a tremendous, almost spiritual, energy in the waterways of his homeland. Skilful use of sibilance in the description of the swooshing 'rushing waters' effectively conveys their restorative, rejuvenating energies.

Feeling the rhythm

The energy of the waters is connected naturally to a different type of cultural energy in the third quatrain, that of music and dance. The poem here expands its vision from the natural beauty of the landscape to the beauty of the 'native' people who enjoy this tropical heaven. In this expanded focus, though, specificity is lost: the intensity of the imagery dims in its vague description, akin more to declarative statements rather than precise sensory description. The sound of the 'fiddle and fife' are not described, even though the effect of these 'dear delicious tunes' is clear: they 'stir the hidden depths' of the listener(s). McKay's use of 'stray' and 'dim remembered' to describe these 'melodies' is clever in suggesting the fogginess of memory; they were heard long ago and only exist now in imperfect but potent snatches of memory. In one way the lack of specificity is useful, as vague powerful music and dance tends towards universalising such a precious treasure trove of native culture: all cultures have these historical 'dim remembered runes' of folk tradition. Perhaps the desire to universalise also explains the unusual instruments the poet recalls, with fiddles and fife more commonly associated with Scotland than with

Jamaica. That explains too, the rather non-specific descriptions of McKay's idealised landscape with its forests, streams and mountains could be almost anywhere. It is as redolent of Scotland or Switzerland as much as it is of Jamaica.

McKay's soundscape is particularly euphonic: there is a beauty to his repetition of soft Ls, Ns and Rs but these are energised by the snappier Ts, Fs and the blunter Ds ('Village dances and dead delicious tunes'). A particularly euphonic choice, the word 'runes' is interesting in its connotations of mystery and deciphering. This word can be used to signify a magical spell or incantation and this seems highly appropriate in this context, given the entrancing effects of the 'village dances' and 'dear, delicious tunes' such folk heritage seems to 'stir' deep in the collective consciousness, something located in the soul rather than the mind.

I will arise and go now and go

McKay's poem is undoubtedly full of an acute longing for home: the poem's insistent repetition of 'I shall return' becoming a plaintive refrain that is easily recognised and understood by any cultural exile. The phrase begins each quatrain and in total is repeated six times, a repetition that underscores the desperation to return. In such a short poem this refrain might lose its edge but McKay cleverly repeats it with a twist; The first line reads 'I shall return again, I shall return' whereas the penultimate line inverts this: 'I shall return, I shall return again'. But the more it is said in the poem, the more the feeling grows that this is just mere wishful thinking rather than determined action.

The reason to actually return is only articulated in the final line and this line is unique in its scansion. McKay adheres to iambic pentameter, or certainly five beats to a line, the whole way through the poem until the final line. Here he adds an extra beat, rendering this line hypermetrical, something he achieves by a skilfully placed caesura after the first 'long in the line i.e.:

'To **ease** | my **mind** | of **long**, | **long years** | of **pain**.'

Home then represents a place of restoration and comfort, a refuge from a hostile world that has caused prolonged suffering. McKay, cleverly leaves this 'pain' open-ended, allowing the poem to connect more universally to all exiles. The journey into the wider world has clearly not been an easy one and the molossus (the three consecutive heavy beats in the line) along with the caesura produce a slow, faltering effect, as if the belief behind the declarative statement is not paper thin. The metrical heaviness of the line suggests a weariness produced by the bruising reality of grinding racism that McKay found commonplace in America.

It is natural to pine for home as a restorative to this existential 'pain', but the reality is that racism was alive and well in Jamaica too. McKay's 'Constab Ballads', also from 1912, explored a darker side of Jamaican life fuelled by McKay's own personal experiences of racism as a policeman in the capital, Kingstown. To push further down this autobiographical line, McKay was perpetually peripatetic, i.e. a compulsive, restless wanderer. Journeying from Jamaica to America to Holland, Belgium, London and Paris, then onto North Africa, and then back to America, he finally finished his days in Chicago. He never returned to Jamaica making this repeated insistence to 'return' no more than a fond nostalgia for a place that perhaps existed only in his mind, but nevertheless helped him cope on his long meanderings through the wider world.

I Shall CRUNCH Again:

RETURN - WONDER - GOLDEN - SAPPHIRE - LOITER - BATHE - DREAMS - RUSHING - FIDDLE - DELICIOUS - NATIVE - MELODIES - RETURN - PAIN

Wilfred Owen, *Disabled*

Owen's war

A young man joining up to fight would have no idea at all what the reality of fighting would have been like. The First World War was the first fully mechanised war, with mustard gas, machine guns, high explosive shells and, latterly, tanks. The nature of trench warfare was profoundly different to battle in previous wars, being essentially a long attritional process. The numbers speak for themselves:

- Eight million soldiers were killed
- Including civilians, about twenty million people died
- On just the first day of the battle of the Somme, twenty thousand men were killed, sixty thousand injured. That's one man dead or injured every second for twenty-four hours.
- Life expectancy of a junior officer was one month.
- Around two million soldiers, sailors and airmen returned to Britian severely disabled in one way of another, with around 40,000 of them amputees.

Wilfred Owen wrote several contradictory things about war and poetry. In his preface to his collection of war poems, for instance, he said he was 'above all…not concerned with Poetry', but that "The Poetry is in the Pity'. By this he was seeking to make a distinction between self-consciously stylised and elevated grand Poetry and the kind of poetry he was writing, which was more grounded in reality, more concerned with truth than style.

Owen also called himself a 'conscientious objector with a very seared conscience'. In other words, he felt deeply ambivalent about the war and his role in it. There was a powerful tension in his character between different conceptions of himself. On the one side was the Christian, poetic self - sensitive, compassionate and romantic, in love with the works of Romantic poets, such as Keats and Shelley. On the other side was the soldierly self; disciplined, manly, ordered, heroic, stoical. Much of Owen's best poet springs from this internal conflict.

Often in Owen's poetry he is angry not so much at the nature or the war itself but at the way propaganda back home misrepresented the reality of warfare for the soldiers. A classic example is his poem *Dulce et Decorum Est* in which he accuses war propagandists of callously spreading the 'old lie' to 'children ardent for some desperate glory' that it is sweet and fitting to die for one's country. Clearly the soldier, whose thoughts and experiences are relayed via a narrator, in *Disabled*, swallowed the same lies and has come to bitterly regret his innocent credulity.

AN APPEAL TO YOU

Give us a hand old man!

Restless shuffling

Throughout this poem Owen mixes structural regularity with irregularity. While a steady pentameter keeps the lines running in a generally iambic pattern, both the rhyme scheme and the stanza form change restlessly from one section to the next. At first things seem fairly regular in a first stanza of six lines and three pairs of full rhymes – 'dark/park', 'grey/day', 'hymn/him'. The last is an example of 'rich' rhyme. Along with the slightly unexpected rhyme pattern – ABACBC – this last rhyme subtly suggests something slightly skewed or off key.

The second stanza has an extra line and immediately deviates from the rhyme scheme established in the first stanza. Some of the rhyme sounds are carried over from the first stanza, such as the first line's 'gay', which has no rhyme pair in the second stanza, but echoes the B rhyme from the first, as well as the 'dim/slim' pair. The rhyme scheme of BDCDCEC introduces a triple rhyme – 'trees/knees/disease' and includes an unrhymed word, 'hands', again creating a subtle effect, here sonically underscoring the idea of a lack of touch or connection.

While the third stanza repeats the seven-line form, the rhyme scheme shifts again. This time there are no rhymes linking back to the previous stanza and the scheme shuffles a little to FGFGHGH. Surprisingly, in the following much longer, sixteen-line stanza, the rhyme pattern falls into a regular cross-rhyme scheme, so that the first and third lines are paired as are the second and fourth. This is more balanced and orderly stanza is succeeded by a much shorter tercet, with the middle rhyme then carried over into the next stanza – 'fruits'/'institutes'. The poem ends in a couplet where the same end word is used instead of the sonic closure a full rhyme would provide. Like 'hands', 'come' is the only other word at the end of a line that doesn't have a rhyme pair. This and the fact that the question remains unanswered, underlines the idea of separation and lonely isolation.

So what, you might ask. What is the significance of this unsettled, restless form? Well, the formal restlessness perhaps embodies the ill-at-easeness of the soldier, reflecting his agitated and unhappy state of mind. The underpinning of the pentameter meanwhile helps to maintain a sense of continuity in a poem that is composed of a series of fragments and could, otherwise, degenerate into bits and pieces. Psychologically, the metre arguably also suggests some enduring strength, an underpinning orderliness, a kind of backbone, a strong spine that helps the soldier to endure. Notably too, the most orderly and regular section of the poem is the stanza entirely devoted to the soldier's fond memories of the past, before he was wounded in battle and then left afterwards to deal with the consequences of a lifetime of disability.

Now and then
Another important structural feature of the poem is how it is arranged in

terms of time. While some sections, such as the first stanza, focus on the present situation of the soldier, others describe his past, while the last stanza looks forward to an unhappy future. The fond, vivid depictions of the soldier's past life make his present suffering more poignant through stark contrasts. The unnamed soldier clearly is an everyman figure and the details of his past are common ones shared by many young men. In particular, he has a vivid memory of girls looking pretty and making flirtatious eye contact with them, 'and girls glanced lovelier', of the feel of their slim waists and the warm touch of female hands. He remembers too playing sport, being 'carried shoulder-high' after a victory at football, the cheers of the crowd after a goal and getting drunk in celebration. He remembers his vanity, his pride in his attractive appearance, the allure of an army uniform with 'jewelled hilts/ For daggers in plaid socks', the promises of camaraderie, the crowds cheering and seeing them off.

These vibrant memories of a happy, vigorous youth are bookended by his situation now in the present and by what is to come. Joie de vivre, vigour and dynamism have been replaced by a miserable, passive, sedentary existence, hollowed out of hope, goals and purpose. While the first stanza pictures him 'sat in a wheeled chair, waiting for dark' with nothing to do other to wait for sleep, the last outlines the bleak prospect of the years ahead:

'… he will spend a few sick years in institutes…
And take whatever pity they may dole'.

And the poem concludes with a sense of frustrated helplessness as the soldier can only wait for someone to come and 'put into bed', like a child or an old man.

Whereas before the war, an artist and various young women found him attractive and he had a girlfriend, Meg, now he believes he will never regain loving intimacy with a woman. If women do happen to touch him, they treat him 'like some queer disease', a simile that dehumanises him and suggests distaste, perhaps even disgust. His grief at the loss of his pride in being an attractive man returns at the end of poem, as he notices 'women's eyes' passing over him to 'strong men that were whole', suggesting that the soldier is plagued by the fear that he may now always be alone. No mention is made now of his girlfriend, Meg. He doesn't feel whole, he doesn't feel like a man. Having lost both legs and one forearm, and with his back permanently crooked, he feels enfeebled. Entirely reliant on others, he has lost all control over his life. Physically and mentally, the war has also aged him prematurely. All his happy youthful innocence has been replaced by feelings of disillusionment, alienation and bitterness, a stultifying trap of feelings from which there seems very little prospect of escape.

Before he threw away his knees

The overwhelming bitterness the soldier feels is made harder to swallow by the sense that he was mislead into fighting and by the perception that

his sacrifice was worthless. Clearly, like many of the young recruits in WWI, this young man had no idea what he was letting himself in for and had no real sense even of what he was fighting for. Ignorant of the geopolitics, and, giddy after a sports victory and fuelled by alcohol, he signed up when too young to fight – 'they wrote his life: aged nineteen' – and then he was carried away by the excitement of looking good in a uniform and by the 'drums and cheers' of the crowds.

Among the most powerful and most hear-rending lines of Disabled are the ones describing how this young man got injured in battle. The euphemistic phrasing of 'he threw away his knees' makes this loss seem like a casual, thoughtless accident, something done without much care, like how you might throw away a good chance of a goal or discard an unwanted piece of rubbish. The active form of the phrase, 'he threw', also makes him seem responsible for this action, rather than the victim of enemy violence, suggesting the young soldier blames himself for his loss, that he did this, stupidly, to himself. Similarly, the line describing how he lost his youth and vigour, his blood, his 'colour', makes this seem careless, rash and pointless:

'He's…/ Poured it down shell-holes till the veins ran dry'

There is no sense here of a noble sacrifice for your country, or of glory or courage, or any of the supposed consolations of battle. What we get instead is an overwhelming sense of bitterness at the waste of a promising life.

Owen chose to write this poem in the third person, even though, as a victim of shellshock, he had spent some time out of the trenches, recuperating as a patient at Craiglockhart hospital, and thus, had first-hand experience to draw upon. Indeed, so badly had the poet suffered that, if he had chosen to, he could have spent the remainder of the war convalescing. What effect, if any, would there be if this poem had been written as a dramatic monologue in the first person?

Perhaps Owen didn't write in first person because this would have entailed appropriating another man's experience. Moreover, to do so may not have felt entirely authentic. And truth and authenticity really mattered to Wilfred Owen. Although he suffered terrible mental trauma as a result of his combat experiences, Owen had remained physically unscathed by warfare. Until, tragically, he was killed, aged only twenty-five, in the last few weeks of the war.

Disabled crunched:

WHEELED – SHIVERED – LEGLESS – SADDENING – PLAY –
MOTHERED – GAY – BUDDED – GIRLS – BEFORE – NEVER –
HANDS – DISEASE – ARTIST – YOUTH – OLD – LOST –
POURED – HALF – SPURTED – LIKED – MATCHES – DRUNK –
JOIN – GOD – MEG – PLEASE – BEG – LIE – GERMANS –
FEARS – JEWELLED – SMART – PAY – ESPIRIT – CHEERS –
SOME – ONLY – SOUL – SICK – RULES – PITY – WOMEN'S –
WHOLE – COLD – WHY

Zulfikar Ghose, *Decomposition*

A good composition

In *Decomposition* by Zulfikar Ghose, the speaker reflects on a photograph that he took in Bombay, which depicts a beggar's suffering and his invisibility to passers-by. Although the speaker initially sees the beggar as an artistic opportunity, he later feels guilt for trivialising the beggar's situation. Ghose's poem provides readers with a poignant exploration of the complex relationship between art and life.

The double meaning in the poem's title, *Decomposition*, immediately captures both the artistic composition of the speaker's photograph and the breakdown of life that the photograph depicts. In the first part of the poem, the focus is on the speaker's more detached observations. He notices that the beggar's 'shadow (is) thrown aside like a blanket'. This dehumanising simile highlights how easily human lives can be neglected, particularly those who face homelessness. This reductive, dehumanising language extends to the speaker's observations of the beggar's limbs, which 'could be cracks in the stone'. The imagery of the earth suggests how the beggar is hardly noticed by those who walk by, with the imagery of 'cracks' conveying a sense of the beggar's vulnerability – and his 'decomposition', to echo the title – as a result of his situation. This is reinforced by the metaphor 'veined into stone, a fossil man'. The beggar's body becomes a part of the land, suggesting a sense of both physical and existential decay. A fossil is preserved remains, and this comparison reflects the unforgiving reality of life for disenfranchised men and women, particularly in India, as well as the indifference of other people to their suffering; he has become simply part of the familiar environment, a reflection of how such familiarity can make any of us blind to the distress of others.

Ghose is a Pakistani American author, and cultural alienation is a theme throughout his work. His first novel, 'The Contradictions' (1966), focuses on the differences between Western and Eastern attitudes and ways of life. This is evident to some extent in this poem, as Ghose highlights the struggles of disenfranchised people in India, there is also perhaps a universal theme for readers of all cultural backgrounds; social injustice is a harsh reality, but people must not become desensitised to the adversity that some individuals face. Moreover, the poet ruefully acknowledges that even those with artistic temperaments and interests, who might be expected to be more sensitive to the distress of others, can lose their empathy even in the process of producing art.

Dehumanising language is employed throughout the poem, a reflection of the continual suffering of the beggar and the continual indifference from passers-by. The fact that the beggar provides 'routes for the ants' journeys, the flies' descents' juxtaposes him with insects, viewed as pests, and of so little significance as to not be noticeable. These images reveal the depth of his suffering as well as his invisibility to others. He is so lowly he is reduced to being defined by his usefulness to tiny insects. In addition, these comparisons convey the speaker's own dismissive and exploitative attitude in the earlier part of the poem. Rather than considering the beggar's emotions and needs, the speaker initially views him with a tone of detachment, as merely a fitting subject for an artwork. This same observational tone extends to the depiction of the crowd, who are 'bemused by a pavement trickster and quite/ indifferent to this very common sight'. The emphatic positioning of the adjective 'indifferent' at the start of the line draws attention to the widespread nature of a kind of emotional apathy and its opposite, the human capacity for true empathy when confronted with experiences beyond our own understanding. In addition, the poet's use of enjambment, here and throughout the poem, structurally conveys the nature of the indifferent crowd, walking past those who are suffering like the beggar without stopping to help. This is also a comment on the social inequality and widespread poverty in India; the beggar is a 'very common sight', a phrase that highlights perhaps why the beggar is hardly noticed by the crowd.

The man in the street

The tone shifts at the poem's volta from distant observation to artistic curiosity. Initially, the speaker saw the beggar as 'a good composition', an echo of the poem's title, and named the photograph, perhaps ironically, as 'The Man in the Street'. The common phrase 'the man in the street' refers to an everyman character whose views reflect ordinary conventional wisdom. Hence, using this title, implies that the ordinary 'man in the street' in India has been reduced to the status of a beggar. Coupled by the way the beggar is reduced to a type, losing his individuality the irony in the title reflects the potentially exploitative nature of art, using human suffering for, in this case, the sake of photographic success. Later the speaker comes to regret his rather detached and exploitative behaviour, with the adverb 'glibly' conveying a sense of guilt for his actions, a rueful recognition that he took advantage of the beggar and his situation. Not just in the photograph's title and, indeed, but throughout the poem, the beggar remains unnamed. This suggests how de-individualising the experience of being homeless can be, but it could also imply that the speaker, like the 'crowd' who walk past him, did nothing to address the beggar's lack of identity. Written in first person, the poem makes the speaker's voice and experience, not the beggar's, its centre. Even in the title of the photograph, the speaker uses the impersonal noun 'man', as we have said, stripping the beggar of any identity.

There is a suggestion, in the closing lines of the poem, that suffering cannot – and should not – be only reduced to art. The speaker reflects on how the beggar is captured in the photograph, with '(h)is head in the posture of one weeping/ into a pillow'. Only on reflection does the speaker acknowledge the beggar's humanity, with the emotive language 'weeping' conveying the speaker's recognition of the beggar's suffering.

This emotional connection contrasts to the start of the poem, where the speaker's attention was focused on coolly cataloguing the physical appearance of the beggar, who was 'grey-haired' and wearing 'shorts and a dirty shirt'. While these examples foreground the speaker's initial objectification of the beggar - his unresponsiveness to the beggar's emotions – his preoccupation with the photographic opportunity that the beggar represents – despite the detached tone of the speaker, the descriptions elicit sympathy from us as readers for the beggar. His age is unknown, and thus his grey hair may be related to growing older, but it could also be representative of the stress that the beggar experiences because of his plight. The adjective 'dirty' also shows the beggar's lack of access to sanitation and basic amenities.

The speaker's guilt becomes apparent in the poem's final line, as the photograph 'chides (him) now for (his)/ presumption at attempting to compose/ art of his hunger and solitude'. This ending encapsulates one of the poem's key themes: the tension between art and exploitation. Whilst photographs can be used to raise awareness about the experiences of marginalised individuals, there is the danger that capturing moments of human suffering for the sake of artistic success may be self-serving and even exploitative. Additionally, aestheticizing such subject matter – making a beautiful-looking photo of someone's suffering – may be a kind of betrayal, anaesthetising the viewer's response to the subject matter. At first, for instance, the speaker valued his photo not because it might incite any action to alleviate this beggar or any other beggars' suffering, but for its artistic, aesthetic quality of being well-composed, a 'good composition'. Whilst social apathy needs to be addressed, it is important not just to represent the beggar but see him as more than a photograph, as flesh and blood. The final word, 'solitude', captures the pain and isolation of living in poverty, and makes us as readers reflect on our own attitudes to artistic representations of human suffering.

Decomposition crunched:

BOMBAY – BEGGAR – GREY-HAIRED – ASIDE – CRACKS – ROUTES – EXHAUSTION – FOSSIL – CROWD – BEMUSED – INDIFFERENT – PAVEMENT – COMPOSITION – GLIBLY – REMARKING- LIVED – WEEPING – CHIDES – PRESUMPTION – ART

Gillian Clarke, *Catrin*

What emotions do you most associate with the adjective 'motherly'? Perhaps take a moment to write a few down. Inevitably, we have certain expectations of how a subject such as motherhood is going to be presented in a work of art and the same too about the relationship between mothers and babies, and also about the relationship specifically between mothers and daughters. When the writer is a woman writing about her own experience, there is a pressure to present oneself in a way that fits these societal expectations, to be seen to be motherly. After all, although Clarke's poem focuses most intently on describing a relationship, it is also a portrait of both Catrin as a character and a self-portrait. We might expect a mother to express feelings of care, gentleness, tenderness, intimacy, wonder, protectiveness and togetherness among other things, especially to a new-born baby, the sort of loving feelings often depicted in images of one the ultimate of all mothers, the Virgin Mary, cradling the Christ child.

Fierce confrontation

Although there are words within the poem that fit conventional ideas of motherly feelings towards a baby or young child, notably these few and far between and are significantly outnumbered by words depicting their relationship as an ongoing, intense battle. True, the word 'love' does crop up twice and so too does the adjective 'tender', once. But even then, love is described through a distancing metaphor as a 'tight red rope', an image of the umbilical cord that suggests being restrained and possibly pain. Moreover, mother and daughter are described as having 'fought over' this object, like violent adversaries. Meanwhile, the warm, soft associations of 'tender' are modulated by being preceded with the adjective 'wild', which implies something desperate and out of control about the speaker's feelings. And, before we get to any of these three words, the relationship between mother and daughter, even before the latter has been born, has already been established as a 'fierce confrontation', a phrase that signals an intense battle between two warriors or two armies. Other words and phrases that characterise the relationship as a confrontation include, 'fought', 'struggle', 'shouted', 'won not lost', 'fighting you off, 'defiant glare', 'tightening about my life' and 'conflict'. If you were Clarke's daughter, Catrin, how would you feel about your mother depicting your relationship as essentially like warfare, and, what is more, in the public forum of a published poem?

Addressing her daughter, the poet presents their relationship as a battle of wills, tracing this battle back to the moment her daughter was born, before that even, to the experience of childbirth, as if the adversarial nature of their relationship was established during that extraordinary, life-giving, life-changing experience. The poet imagines the baby's struggle to be born and its crying as expressions of a desperate desire for independent selfhood:

'We want, we shouted,
To be two, to be ourselves.'

It's a startling idea when you think of how helpless newborn babies are and of how they more usually cry to be comforted and to be fed. In other words, Clarke's reading of the situation is a projection of her own feelings – the baby did not shout this, because babies don't shout. Nor are they born speaking words, of course. Hence this imagining of the baby's feelings says more about the poet's character than about her daughter's.

The upper hand

In this battle for wills, is one character dominant and the other dominated? And does the power relationship stay the same or change as the poem unfolds and the daughter grows from baby to a girl on the cusp of her teenage years? Ostensibly, as we would expect, the mother appears, initially, to be in charge and in control. She's the narrator, so it's her voice we hear. She is relating her memories, selecting and describing these experiences from her perspective and we don't hear directly from the daughter at all; she is voiceless. Additionally, the first and more substantial of the two stanzas is dominated by the mother. The speaker has the power to 'remember' something her daughter cannot, so she has the upper hand in terms of knowledge of the situation, an advantage emphasised by the repetition of 'I **can** remember'. Additionally, from the start the daughter is addressed not by her name, but as a 'child', underscoring her youth and inexperience as well as her dependence on the speaker. Significantly the pronoun 'I' also appears more frequently in this stanza than 'you' or, indeed, 'we'.

But there seems to be a powershift in the second stanza. In this shorter, less substantial second stanza there's only one 'I' pronoun and one 'my' compared to four 'yous' and two 'yours'. Additionally, more of the lines in this stanza describe the daughter than her mother and Clarke seems to be on the backfoot, under siege, on the defensive: 'Still I am fighting/ You off', as if the daughter is attacking and has the advantage. There is even an image of strangulation, with the 'old rope' described as potentially fatally 'tightening about' the poet's 'life', like a noose. Rather than concluding with the mother's answer, this stanza also ends with the daughter's desires, left unresolved.

Tender circles

The stanza began, however, with the claim of a score draw in the battle between mother and daughter. Tracing all the pronouns in the poem seems to confirm that they are, indeed, a good match for each other, with an equal number of first person and second person pronouns. Moreover, pronouns that link mother and daughter, suggesting a shared identity or common characteristics at least, significantly outnumber those that separate them: 'We', 'our', 'ourselves', 'us' feature almost twice as often as the first or second person pronouns. The implication that the daughter is a mini mirror image of her mother is also conveyed in several other ways, perhaps most notably at the end of the first stanza, in the two lines we've already quoted when the poet imagines them wanting and doing the same thing. While the overt meaning of these lines is about the desire for separate identities, they share the same desire and the repeated 'we' and the final word 'ourselves' bring the two characters together, an effect underscored by doubling, both of words and phrases - 'we...' and 'we...' and 'to be...' and 'to be...'.

Although there are sporadic rhymes, Clarke's poem is close to speech. It is like a speech in a piece of drama, impassioned, strikingly bold and frank, unsentimental, with a handful of vivid and colourful metaphors, especially the central one of love as a red rope, and a strong sense of character and place. Without a regular metre and fitting no conventional traditional form, Catrin is close to a piece of spoken word poetry, written as much for the ear as the eye. In it a mother addresses us, the readers, putting us in the position of a daughter who is growing up fast and beginning to demand choice and freedom and independence. The poem presents but doesn't resolve the mother's dilemma. Giving in to the demand to stay out 'in the dark' could be the start of a slippery slope. Cave in and more, bigger demands will follow. On the other hand, being too restrictive might create resentment, even, eventually incite rejection and rebellion, damaging their relationship. Such are the tricky dilemmas of parenthood, and such are the inevitable complexities of growing up and becoming an independent self.

Catrin crunched:

CHILD – I – WATCHING – PEOPLE – TRAFFIC – REMEMBER –
CONFRONTATION – LOVE – FOUGHT – DISINFECTED –
WROTE – WALLS – WORDS – CIRCLES - STRUGGLE –
SEPARATE – OURSELVES – STRUGGLE – CLOUDED –
FIGHTING – YOU – STRONG – ROSY – GLARE – ROPE
TIGHTENING – CONFLICT – ASK – DARK

Beatrice Garland, *Kamikaze*

Kamikaze

A horde of Mongol ships, hungry for destruction, led by the immortal Kublai Khan approaches the shores of Japan. Stranded and seeking a safe vantage from which to launch their attack they lie in wait. A matter of time. Nature, a force in Japan so often malevolent and so often injudicious was, however, to intervene. And its intervention was decisive. The vengeful 1281 typhoon that swept the Mongols from the sea was christened a kamikaze or 'divine wind.' The Mongols were never to attack Japan again.

Although the Mongol fleet was never to be seen again, the sound of the divine wind was to echo through the history of Japan. It whistled through the air towards the American ships as they massed in the water around Japan, it was to be heard in the deafening detonation of the atomic bombs over Nagasaki and Hiroshima and in the poem *Kamikaze* by Beatrice Garland.

Garland once said she would 'spend a lot of the day listening to other people's worlds'. This secret ear for the inner workings and motivations of others is the skill that allows her to unpick the 'powerful incantations' that drive the poem's principal character, the pilot, towards the sea. The poem hints at clues that led to the entanglement of self-destruction and honour: 'a samurai sword', a 'huge flag waved' and 'little fishing boats'. Each image presents the three conflicting drives in the mind of the pilot. The sword is symbolic of the Bushido code of honour, a simple life and self-sacrifice, the flag in its infinite waving loop references a deep unfathomable patriotism and the fishing boats evoke the pastoral beauty and oceanic tradition of the paintings of Hokusai.

If an 'incantation' is a powerful pattern of phrase repeated again and again, then these images of honour, tradition and loyalty have been repeated often throughout the history of Japan. Like the poem their message has passed from generation to generation leaving its lasting imprint. The children in the poem 'learn' from a process of emotional osmosis and become a simulacrum of their parents. As the lines and stanzas enjamb into each other so too do the attitudes as they are passed onwards.

What we are led then to question what is the real weapon in the poem: the destructive potential of the Kamikaze pilot or the 'incantations' that send him plunging towards the sea, the divine wind come once again to save Japan from the aggressor. Neither? And what is true bravery here? To sacrifice your life unthinkingly for emperor or country, or to go against indoctrination and face down the bitter scorn of society?

Noble sacrifice

The rich 'Bushido' or Samurai tradition of self-sacrifice, loyalty and simple life inspire awe rather than revulsion as, very often, has the destructive power of the seas (take a look at Hokusai's The Wave). So, what is being criticised in the poem? Why are we meant to empathise with the pilot, why 'must' we feel his emotions as he performs his noble and yet devastating sacrifice? Much like Alfred Lord Tennyson's famous Crimean war poem The Charge of the Light Brigade, Wilfred Owen's WWI poem Disabled and Simon Armitage's more modern Remains, the poem functions as a critique of the propaganda that piggybacked on venerable traditions. The chance to become a Kamikaze offers a 'one-way journey into history'. Here we see the classic diction of propaganda. The semantic field of adventure tells us this is a fairy story that has been sold to these men in order that they so willingly 'embark[ed]' on their 'journey'. Yet the pilot loses no dignity in the opening stanza when he carries his 'samurai sword' as if he is some spiritual successor to the noble Bushido. Yet this young man is only sent with 'enough' fuel for a one-way trip. The juxtaposition of his youth and sense of adventure cuts sharply against the deadly fuel allowance of the regime who have cruelly counted out his remaining time on earth out in aviation fuel. They certainly aren't accounting for the pilot's ultimate decision to return home. Returning as he does, despite the half empty tank, adds a sense of defiance and a different kind of bravery to the one traditionally expected by the parents who greet him on his return.

An ear for other worlds

Stanza two again emphasises the ear we need for the worlds of others. We, and the persona's children, are asked to believe that he 'must' have looked down upon the sea. And the sea, so pivotal in the life of an island nation, in this story reflects flashes of his own life before his eyes. The 'dark shoals' of fish become figurative for the 'flag' which in itself reflects his own indecision being 'waved one way, then the other'; the little boats become a fragment of childhood 'bunting' or perhaps the memory of a military parade while the 'flashing silver' of the tuna are the kamikaze who fly with him.

It is these same pilots who are the 'brothers' referenced in stanza three. The 'cairns' they built are ancient markers; it could suggest that his 'brothers' followed the traditional, 'ancient' mindset, and that he is the exception; one who values his own individualism in the face of death. Yet we could also look at these 'cairns' as metaphors for withstanding the 'turbulent inrushes' and impulse to war and destruction. However, we view them, we have to read a critique of the prevailing wisdom of the time. The stanza lacks punctuation and becomes an 'incantation' to cherishing life. The infinite loop ∞ of the flag, representing the perpetual cycle of war and destruction, is rejected and replaced with the sibilant sounds of the ocean and ever onrushing waves. The pilot returns to land like everything else, 'shore, salt-sodden…awash' and yet also remarkably colourful. 'Crabs', 'mackerel', 'prawns' which are 'butt marked' and 'feathery'. Amongst this plethora of life affirming imagery and debris from the sea the pilot is returned to land '-safe', his bounty hanging like decorative medals.

Reborn, the hero returns to the shore. He has fought off the 'breakers' of predominant wisdom, turned from the infinite cycle of destruction and defied the half-empty tank he was sent on his 'journey' with. Yet he is now a 'dark prince… dangerous' a negative influence to be shunned. The semantic field of shame tells us of a culture that isn't ready to accept this new form of anti-conformist heroism. The defiance of the older generation eventually seeps through to the young who too avoid their grandfather as 'chatter' and 'laughter' turns to 'silence'. It seems clear, that we, as readers, are being asked to scorn the parents whose attitudes are thrown into sharp contrast with the colourful man who emerges from the sea. Thus the 'silence' at the end of the poem is remarkably free from any form of condemnation and an opportunity for the reader to make up their own mind, unlike the children who had it made for them.

Of course, the cycle of destruction, like a great wave, will pass over one man. The bombs that fell on Japan in 1945 were another destructive and divine wind. The controversial shrines or 'cairns' that pay homage to the bravery of the kamikaze are still visited in droves by tourists. What then is the message of the poem? It is illusive in many respects and problematised by the fact that we will never truly know what caused the pilot to abandon his mission. Was it the visions of beauty; the endless wealth of the ocean? Or was it cowardice? This distance is highlighted by the third person perspective we get in the first stanzas. This perspective is full of colour and imagery and when we finally switch to the first person the language becomes solemn, almost shameful of the act of shaming itself.

Kamikaze crunched:

EMBARKED – SAMURAI – SHAVEN – POWERFUL – ONE-WAY – HISTORY – HALF – CHILDREN – LOOKED – LITTLE – STRUNG – SEA – ARCING – FLAG – EIGHT – DARK – FLASHING – SUN – REMEMBERED – WAITING – CAIRNS – WITHSTOOD – TURBULENT – FATHER'S – GRANDFATHER'S – AWASH – CLOUD-MARKED – BLACK – SILVER – DANGEROUS – BACK – MOTHER – EYES – NEIGHBOURS – EXISTED – CHILDREN – LEARNED – SILENT – RETURNED – LOVED – WONDERED – DIE

Seamus Heaney, *Blackberry-Picking*

Innocence and experience

Blackberry-picking was published in Seamus Heaney's celebrated, broadly autobiographical first collection of poetry, 'Death of a Naturalist' in 1966. Despite appearances, the title of this collection doesn't refer to the death, perhaps by murder, of David Attenborough or such similar famous naturalist, but, rather, to a symbolic death; the 'death' of an innocent, perhaps naïve, fascination with nature within the mind of young Heaney as he develops from child to adolescent to adult. In many of the poems in 'Death of a Naturalist' the childish joy and excitement the innocent narrator feels in his encounters with nature becomes tempered by the discovery of darker, more disturbing dimensions, both within nature and inside the narrator himself, particularly as he begins to grow-up and become more experienced.

The dramatization in the collection of a shift of perspective from childish innocence to more adult experience recalls the famous songs of William Blake, while the depictions of the natural world, especially as a source for poetic inspiration reflects the influence of other Romantic poets, particularly William Wordsworth, whose lines, from his autobiographical epic, 'The Prelude', 'fair seedtime had my soul, and I grew up/ Fostered alike by beauty and by fear' Heaney quotes admiringly in his selected poems of 1966-1987. However, Heaney was always keen to point out that he was Irish, not an English poet, with strong roots in the culture and the landscape of Ireland, an essential quality reflected in a poetic voice with Irish, not English, cadences.

Advancements of learning

In many of the poems in 'Death of a Naturalist', Heaney learns life-lessons from encounters with the natural world. The immediately preceding poem, for instance, is called An Advancement of Learning, and features Heaney as a boy downfacing his fears, as embodied in a slimy rat. In the poems immediately after Blackberry-Picking, Heaney discovers the importance of labour, perseverance and teamwork in the making of butter, and, in The Early Purges, remembers how he was 'purged' of sentimentality towards animals when as a six-year-old he witnessed the drowning of unwanted kittens in a bucket, drawing the tough conclusion that 'on well-run farms pests have to be kept down'. What life-lesson does the narrator learn from their experience in Blackberry-Picking?

Certainly, the narrator learns that everything that exists is subject to change, that nothing stays the same, particularly over time, even nature's bounty, and that, however much we might hope otherwise, there's nothing any of us can do to stop this process. But the experience with the blackberries suggests more than that, doesn't it? It's not just a process of change the speaker witnesses, it's one, specifically, of decay, of rot, even of corruption, with something precious and wonderful, the berries which have been 'hoarded' like a treasure, a 'cache', transforming into something vile and disgusting. Heaney uses sensory and figurative imagery to generate feelings of revulsion: The unpleasantly tactile 'fur' of the 'fungus' is described visually as 'rat-grey', recalling Heaney's horror of rats in The Advancement of Learning and in other poems. Additionally, this furry fungus is personified as greedily 'glutting' on the fruit, like some malign, ravenous parasite. Consequently, the sweet juice was 'stinking', adding an olfactory dimension to the nausea-inducing disgustingness.

Summer's blood

Heaney's early poetry was particularly lauded for the poet's ability to evoke the richness physicality of the natural world. In *Blackberry-Picking*, Heaney uses sensory imagery to bring the textures of the physical world vividly to life. The blackberries, for instance, are described both visually as 'glossy and purple' and through tactile imagery as 'hard as a knot'. Collectively, the blackberries become 'big dark blobs' that look, unnervingly, 'like a plate of eyes'. Taste is evoked in the reference to the 'sweet' flesh of the berries that is like 'thickened wine', a simile that combines taste with touch. A sense of taste is also evoked later when this sweetness turns 'sour'. A little internal rhyme in 'briars scratched' sonically evokes their scratchiness, while the tinny sound of the berries hitting the bottom of milk-cans and other receptacles is conjured by 'tinkling'. The sensation of touch is again induced at the end of the stanza through the description of hands being 'peppered' and their palms 'sticky'. Meanwhile, in the second stanza, the rat-grey fur combines visual and tactile imagery, whilst, 'stinking' is olfactory, as is the 'smell of rot'.

While Heaney's liberal of use sensory imagery suggests his joy and pleasure in sensations evoked by direct physical contact with the natural world, a darker undercurrent runs through the poem. The word that first hints at a troubling subtext is 'clot' in the third line. Although, primarily, this is visual and tactile image, evoking the shape and stickiness of the blackberry, the most common association of the word is with 'blood', and 'blood-clots' can, of course, cause serious medical problems. 'Blood' itself appears only a few lines later, with the juice of the fruit described as 'summer's blood', as if the season is alive and its body has been wounded in some way. The reference to 'flesh' tasting 'sweet' adds to an uneasy sense that the speaker is somehow predatory and even carnivorous, hungrily consuming nature's unprotected body. 'Lust' adds an unnervingly sexual dimension to the sensual excitement as well as a sense of excess, while 'stains upon the tongue' carries connotations of guilt and perhaps punishment for a transgression. The simile of the 'plate of eyes' we have already mentioned as adding to an underlying sense of unease. The fact that the blackberries 'burned/ Like a plate eyes' introduces a sense of danger.

Like the 'stains', the sticky hands might also indicate crime and guilt, particularly as these are then connected via a simile to the monstrous fairy tale figure of Bluebeard.

In the *Bluebeard* fairy tale by Charles Perrault, the titular character murders a series of wives and hides their corpses in his castle. When a new wife arrives, he gives her keys to his castle and then leaves her alone to discover the wonders of the place. But before leaving, he tells her there is one key she must not use and one room she must never enter, under any conditions, on pain of death. So, this is a classic temptation scenario and, inevitably, in the end, of course, the young wife enters the forbidden room. Horrified by what she discovers there, she drops the keys in a pool of blood and then hears her husband stomping down the corridor to exact the promised punishment. Presumably, Bluebeard's palms are 'sticky' with blood and/or with sin and guilt. Certainly, the allusion to this tale of temptation, transgression, sin and bloody punishment adds significantly to the poem's network of unease.

Fostered alike by beauty and by fear

Where does it come from, this undercurrent of darkness? Why does Heaney seem to feel that his ostensibly innocent picking and eating of blackberries had such troubling undertones?

Running parallel with ideas of the natural world as place of inspiration, sanctuary and bounty, there is a long tradition in Romantic poetry of unease about man's interactions with mother nature and the destructive passions this interaction can, sometimes, unleash. While in poems such as *I Wandered Lonely as a Cloud*, Wordsworth finds simply joy and comfort in nature, in other poems, such as *Nutting*, published in 1800, he discovers much darker feelings. In this poem, the poet describes how as young man, having stumbled across an untouched clearing, a 'dear nook', a 'virgin scene', feeling 'voluptuous' and jealous of any 'rivals', he despoils this special secluded place with sudden explosive violence. After leaving the 'mutilated bower', feeling exulted 'beyond the wealth of kings', the poet just as suddenly feels as a sense of pain, perhaps of shame, as if nature is chastising him for his crimes against her. In another famous example from *The Prelude* (1850), Wordsworth similarly imagines the hills of the Lake District rising above his boyish self to admonish him for another boyhood transgression, this time the stealing of a small boat.

The narrative of the titular poem of Heaney's first collection has distinct Wordsworthian echoes. In it, a young boy steals frogspawn from a 'flax-dam' to put into jars and watch the frogs develop. Some time later, perhaps when the boy has grown up a little more, when he returns to the flax-dam, the frogs seem to be angry at him and the atmosphere has become threatening: 'The air' is 'thick with a bass chorus'; the frogs are 'cocked' like 'grenades' and want 'vengeance'. If he puts his hand into the water, the boy knows that 'the spawn would clutch it'. Understandably, feeling scared and sickened, he 'turned and ran'.

In *Blackberry-Picking* there is a similar, though less pronounced, sense that mother nature is teaching the young male speaker an important moral lesson. His excessive greed and lust for the fleshy berries he plunders seems to be punished by his 'cache' turning 'sour'. Is there a sexual dimension and perhaps a religious significance to this experience? Probably yes to both. The sensual pleasures the boy experiences could shade into subconsciously sexual feelings, while the excessive love of the physical world, a fallen world that is subject to decay, might, from a Christian perspective, suggest a lack of proper attention to the spiritual and eternal. Additionally, the narrative of picking fruit inevitably re-calls the Garden of Eden, particularly as the reference to Bluebeard makes us think of stories of temptation, transgression and punishment.

Not quite in harmony

Heaney's poem is almost, but not quite, written in heroic couplets, viz paired lines of iambic pentameter that finish with full end rhymes. Although all the lines in *Blackberry-Picking* are written in a slightly roughened iambic pentameter and they are arranged in paired lines and finish too with end rhymes, nearly all of these are half-rhymes, or slighter rhymes. Examples of half-rhymes include, 'and sun'/ 'ripen'; 'lust for'/ hunger', while pairs such as 'sweet'/ 'it' and 'jam-pots'/ 'our boots' more weakly echo each other. The exceptions are the full rhymes 'clot'/ 'knot' and the last one, 'rot'/ 'not', with the latter helping to bring the poem to an emphatic close that sounds almost proverbial. In a poem exploring man's, or at least a boy's, relationship with nature, this form suggests a kinship between the two, but also creates a subtle sense of difference, generating a slight sense of dissonance, a subtle sonic contribution to the pervasive undercurrent of unease.

Blackberry-Picking crunched:

AUGUST – RIPEN – CLOT – RED – FLESH – BLOOD – STAINS – HUNGER – US – SCRATCHED – POTATO-DRILLS – FULL – TINKLING – BURNED – EYES – BLUEBEARD'S – HOARDED – FUR – RAT-GREY – STINKING – SOUR – FAIR – ROT – KNEW

Carol Ann Duffy, *War Photographer*

In a famously distressing photograph from the Vietnam War a group of children are pictured running towards the camera and away from a napalm attack that has left the background of the photo a blaze of fire and smoke. (Napalm was an anti-personal weapon, a flammable liquid that stuck to the skin when it ignited.) To the left in the foreground a young boy's distraught expression conveys the horror and trauma of the attack. In the middle, a young, naked girl runs out of the picture, towards us, crying. She is clearly terrified and in agony, with napalm burns all over her body. Her burns were, in fact, so bad doctors did not think she could possibly survive. Thankfully she did.

Imagine you are the photographer who took that picture. Whilst it might be a natural human instinct to immediately run to the aid of this young girl, it is your job to document these events as they unfold and report them as a neutral-as-possible observer. Could you do a job like this, which requires you to suppress your natural empathy for the suffering of others? That photograph had far-reaching consequences; through its publication the Western world was brought face-to-face with the devastating effect of Napalm on innocent civilians, and it helped fuel public opinion against the Vietnam war. The use of such a weapon is now against international law.

Carol Ann Duffy was inspired to write *War Photographer* due to her friendship with two well respected war photographers, Don McCullin and Philip Jones Griffiths. She was interested in the difficulties these men faced when they witnessed such horrific moments in human history and were forced to attempt to capture them for the 'consumption' of the media in the Western world. Whilst the Vietnam image may have inspired a public outcry in 1972, Duffy explores the notions that our sympathy for those depicted is fleeting, and the proliferation of images of war-torn nations has ultimately desensitised all or us to the extent that we simply 'do not care'.

The observer & the observed

Duffy chooses to use a third person narrative perspective throughout, creating the impression that 'the War Photographer' of the title is the subject under scrutiny. There is a clear irony here, as the observer becomes the observed; the poetic voice scrutinises the intimate moments of the photographer in his dark room, revealing his inner turmoil when he 'is finally alone'.

The intimate knowledge the narrator has of the photographer's thoughts gives the reader the impression that the photographer's mind is turning inwards; he appears to be scrutinising his role in creating these 'spools of suffering' - the sibilance here perhaps reinforcing his sense of disgust. The fragmented sentence structures are like a stream of consciousness: 'Belfast. Beirut. Phnom Penh', as if his mind is flashing back to the war-torn locations almost involuntarily.

Ordinary pain

The sequence of flashbacks is brought to life with the final sentence of the first stanza 'all flesh is grass'. This is a much-quoted biblical phrase used to refer to the transitory nature of life: ultimately when we die our flesh is returned to the earth and feeds into the cycle of life. Used in this context the image could reflect the way the photographer is attempting to comfort himself and rationalise the distress and death he is witnessing. The reference to 'flesh' could refer to the nakedness of the victims (linking to the picture of the Vietnam girl); their indignity overwhelms him and covers the images quite literally like a landscape of grass. Reminding himself of this saying is an example of the way he attempts to separate his own emotional responses from what he is witnessing, but this becomes increasingly difficult as the poem progresses.

There is a juxtapositioning throughout the poem of the suffering experienced by the people in the war-torn communities and the mundane lives of those in 'Rural England'. Statements such as 'simple weather can dispel' our 'ordinary pain' and that the 'fields' of England don't 'explode beneath the feet of running children' emphasise the gulf between these experiences. We take the peace and security of our land for granted, and the image of running children is particularly powerful in evoking a sense of the vulnerability and innocence of many of those caught up in these war zones. Once again, the Vietnam image of the running girl is evoked, particularly within the last phrase of the stanza: 'nightmare heat' with its suggestions of napalm. Coupled with the reference to flesh in the last phrase of the opening stanza, we cannot fail to make the connection with the burning skin of children. Duffy's use of imagery combined with careful structuring is hugely powerful and evocative, bringing home to the reader both what the civilians in battlegrounds experience, and how the war photographer struggles to cope with bearing witness to it.

Trembling & control

Duffy adopts the traditional iambic pentameter throughout most the poem, a metre often reserved for heavyweight subjects. However, there are key moments where she deviates from the pattern. Line two of stanza one, for example, contains an additional iamb, reflecting how the 'spools of suffering' are too great to be contained within the line. The line therefore becomes iambic hexameter, also known as an alexandrine. In line four of stanza one the opposite happens; only four iambs are used. In contrast to the over-spilling of suffering in line two, Duffy here could be highlighting the inadequacy the photographer feels his dark room offers as a place of sanctity to develop these images of the end of human life.

The four regular stanzas each consisting of exactly six lines reflect the photographer's desire to maintain order and control over his emotions. This idea is further evident in the 'ordered rows' he uses to lay out his images. The rhyme scheme is also reassuringly regular, with a rhyming couplet in lines two and three and five and six of each stanza. However, the fact that lines one and four do not tie in with this neat, ordered pattern reflects that despite his best efforts, the photographer is not able to fully maintain regimented control, over suffering, over his emotions and over the effect of his photos. This ties in with the 'tremble' that creeps into his hands, as he attempts to remind himself that 'he has a job to do.'

The second stanza starts abruptly. A matter-of-fact tone is swiftly established, as the photographer attempts to jolt his mind back to the more mundane tasks of the present, where 'solutions slop in trays'. Again, however, the sibilance which creeps into this phrase highlights his disgust, and reveals the trembling of his hands. This time as he thinks of the present, the sentence fragment 'Rural England' also carries a sense of distaste, perhaps even bitterness. 'Home again' follows. Any comfort is, however, very short-lived. Just a couple of metrical beats later and his mind turns to the contrast between the 'ordinary pain' felt here with the suffering felt by the 'running children' who are the subjects of his photographs.

The start of the third stanza contrasts with the start of the second. Whereas at that point he had been attempting to force himself to focus on the task at hand, this time the statement 'Something is happening' demonstrates that he has now been irrevocably drawn into the world of his photographs. The development of the photographs is of course what the photographer is aiming to do, but the process of the development of one picture in particular absorbs him completely; whilst the subject of the picture is a 'stranger' to him (the phrase perhaps highlighting the attitude he typically takes towards his subjects), the way in which this becomes a 'half-formed ghost' reflects the ghostly nature of the image, and hints towards the fact that this man is no longer alive. This is confirmed as his mind turns to 'the cries of this man's wife' and how the 'blood stained into the foreign dust'.

They do not care

The final stanza acts as a moment of realisation for the war photographer; the pain of a single man in the previous stanzaexpands into 'a hundred agonies', emphasising that the shot he captured is a drop in the ocean of suffering he witnesses. Emotive language is juxtaposed with the more factual 'in black and white', bringing us to the perspective of his editor who merely sees the images as a product he is packaging for consumption within 'Sunday's supplement' of his paper. There is a bitterness in the subsequent reference to the reader's response, as although their 'eyeballs prick with tears', this is a fleeting moment quickly forgotten as they move on to their comfortable lives and their 'pre-lunch beers'. The trite internal rhyme reinforces the sense of the photographer's disdain. The narrative perspective finally brings us back to the point of view of the photographer who gazes 'impassively', emotionally disconnected, out of the aeroplane window at his own country where 'they do not care' about his work nor the suffering he is paid to witness for us.

War Photographer crunched:

FINALLY – SUFFERING – RED – CHURCH – PRIEST – FLESH – JOB – TREMBLE – HOME – DISPEL – EXPLODE – NIGHTMARE – HAPPENING – TWIST – GHOST – APPROVAL – MUST – BLOOD – AGONIES – EDITOR – SUPPLEMENT – BEERS – IMPASSIVELY – CARE

Jackie Kay, *Dusting the Phone*

Have you ever met a person with a pressing problem, who no matter how many solutions you offer, seems to find a way to render each one useless, and, exasperated, you finally find yourself thinking, hmmm, think the person is the problem here? Welcome to *Dusting the Phone* by Jackie Kay. Scottish-Nigerian Kay manages, though, to eventually rescue her poetic persona, allowing the reader to feel sympathy for, rather than infuriation with, this garrulous speaker. This poem, from her 1993 collection 'Other Lovers', resonates strongly with Elizabeth Barret Browning's *Sonnet 29* in its obsessive fixation on an absent lover and the strength of its latent erotic charge.

Hanging on the telephone

Prepare for a sudden swoop back to a distant past where phones were not only wired but fixed, where waiting for a phone call could only happen in one place, not myriad locations, where communication response times seem positively glacial compared to 2025. (Un)luckily, the same feelings of powerless desperation, fears of ghosting and need for external validation all remain! It doesn't take much to see how far, and yet how little, we've travelled since 1993: different tech, same problems. The first striking thing about Kay's poem is its emotional intensity ('Come on, damn you') married to a distinctly colloquial style ('I try. It doesn't work'). The whole poem has a spoken ring to it, a linguistic simplicity that fuels a torrential outpouring barely contained by the poem's tercets. The line lengths are long but variable, written in an unrhymed, unpredictable free verse, which gives the poem great, shifting energies and emotional surges, ranging from lonely accusation, powerless desperation to naked sexual frustration.

In one sense, the poem could be viewed as a dramatic monologue of sorts, a speech where the speaker's personality is unknowingly revealed by what is said. So, what does the speaker in this poem reveal about themselves? From the off, their words suggest an intense, extreme personality prone to catastrophising, or at the very least, over-analysing. The first stanza shows a marked discrepancy between reality ('the best that *has been* happening') and how that reality is remoulded in the speaker's mind ('the worst that *could be* happening'). Anaphora ('spending my time') signals a mind circling and circling, unable to escape unhealthy fixations. In a way there is a wilful masochism in the speaker's declarations: they know 'this is not a good idea' yet seem powerless to break free from it. This reading against the grain of reality by assuming the worst is continued into tercet two with its effective repetitions of 'disaster' and 'sirens' which signal high drama. Bizarrely, the speaker assumes a crisis if the phone rings or not.

This pessimistic over-analysing resurfaces in the fourth stanza: 'I go over and over our times together, re-read them'. Notably, the speaker chooses to 're-read' three times rather that remember them and equally noteworthy this is the only instance in the poem where the speaker talks of being part of a couple, through the possessive pronoun 'our', betraying a complete lack of faith in the viability of the romance. In stark contrast, a strategy of separation is revealed in the use of pronouns overall: a pained and aggrieved direct address ('you'/'your') is used five times compared to a massive twenty instances of the first-person pronoun 'I' or 'my'. What does this reveal about the speaker? Simply that they are deeply insecure about their self-worth in a relationship, fuelling, or even perhaps because of, their obsessive tendencies. In fact, the speaker seems to be self-fixated and burdened by a severe victim complex. That or they're just very lonely in a cold, uncaring world.

Caesuras, pauses, in the poetic lines, feature prominently in the second tercet, a poetic technique that characterises the poem more generally: 'In which case, who would ring to tell me? Nobody knows'. On an emotional level, these constant, unpredictable pauses, suggest a mind tortured and unable to find the right words to express the intensity of their pain. The speaker's mind is uncertain, lurching in different directions haphazardly, seemingly incapable of finding solace or answers of any type, barely even able to find the right words to articulate their frenzied uncertainties. Nowhere is this more intense than in the final tercet's final line: 'Come on, damn you, ring me. Or else. What?'. Combined with the long, unpredictable line lengths, (ranging wildly from 19 syllables to 4 syllables but averaging around 13) these multiple caesuras create lines broken up into short sentences and fragments of sentences, generating a powerful staccato delivery. This intense staccato effect is most potent in the third and seventh tercets, i.e. 'A marriage. A full house. One night per week' or 'I am trapped in it. I can't move. I want you'. Here an impatient mind is alternating wildly as it tries to impose control on an essentially uncontrollable entity: the lover.

Opposites attract?

This inability to control the uncontrollable, reflects a wider strategy of clashing opposites. Fundamentally, the lovers seem mismatched: the speaker is fixated on love and the long-term future, the lover embraces the present ('Forget tomorrow') and would rather not 'mention love', clearly preferring to embrace physical pleasures. In the opening tercet, Kay shows the speaker wracked between irreconcilable oppositions. They cannot savour what *is* happening but are driven demented by what *could* be happening, unable to distinguish between *actual* best and *potential* worst. This juxtaposition of opposites is seen most intriguingly in the contrast between the colloquial simplicity of the majority of the poem and the two instances of highly figurative language in tercets three and five.

Tercet three is preoccupied with the future and it's a bracingly figurative future, jolting us from the disaster 'sirens' and guilty declarations of the previous two tercets. The future, like the entire poem, is comprised of binary extremes: it's either heaven or hell. It begins with an enigmatic metaphor: 'the future is a long-gloved hand'. What does this intriguing statement mean? Is it a positive or a negative statement? Long gloves have connotations of opulence, of formal evening wear, so it suggests a future full of prosperity. This, of course, makes the subsequent statement even more abrupt. Suddenly the future is instead 'an empty cup', a sudden swerve from plenitude to poverty. It is a brilliantly concise metaphor, suggesting a future of emptiness and destitution, visualising a beggar's cup, pleading to survive. To keep the reader completely disorientated, Kay provides another vision of the future, the one she really wants: 'A marriage. A full house' - the standard marriage plus children dream. But a complete opposite crashes into this, reflecting the speaker's careening, unstable thought processes. The next vision of the future is 'one night per week /in stranger's white sheets,' a future promising random, one-night sexual liaisons, yet strangely as cold and blank as the white sheets it visualises. There really is no in-between with this speaker: it's all or nothing.

You say it worst when you say nothing at all

The speaker claims to 'assault the postman for a letter', surely a hyperbolic claim, but one conveying the tortured craving for validation that communication promises. The silence is not just deafening, but exasperating. Kay employs a sharp but cruel sense of humour, describing her speaker's cravings as akin to addiction. The acute desperation of the speaker is shown in the statement 'This very second I am waiting on the phone'. Kay plays with the polysemantic possibilities of the verb 'waiting', capturing its most obvious meaning but also the idea of waiting as serving provider. This cleverly suggests a power dynamic in the couple with the speaker subservient to the silent lover's aloof power. Kay leans into the joke, suggesting the speaker will trade for contact, promising 'silver service' in return for a soft word, any word at all. The promise to 'give it extra in return for your call' veers dangerously close to the speaker becoming a type of cliched call-girl, adopting the persona of a sexy maid, exciting but also pathetic, to lure the lover into making contact. It's quite silly but also very sad.

The speaker's pain is not alleviated as the love object continues playing hard-to-get and reality conspires against them: sending 'hoaxes, wrong numbers;/ or worse calls from boring people'. Again, note the agitated

caesuras as well as the booming assonance of the repeated Os, which reflect the speaker's feeling of being assailed by reality. The line is also notably cacophonous: the harsh X/Cs, the aggressive Ps and dull Bs, all enhancing the feelings of frustration. Whereas a phone call would bring freedom of expression and new possibilities, all the speaker gets is its opposite: silence. And then the narrowing of possibilities as the lover's 'voice disappears into my lonely cotton sheets'. This echo of the previous blank sheets of future one-night stands, from tercet three, creates yet another mental circling, connecting back to the swirling destructive thoughts that characterise this speaker.

This is the end?

Kay refuses to grant resolution to the central problem in the poem, refuses to grant a happy ending. Rather than clarifying or even soothing the speaker's anxieties, they are intensified. The final tercet is awful to read, which really dispels any irritation the reader may have felt towards the speaker. The overloading of caesuras (11, counting the end stops) again captures the speaker's frantic, racing thoughts and wild emotional surges, veering wildly from entrapment and powerlessness ('I am trapped in it. I can't move.') to intense desire ('I want you. All the time.') to self-pity ('This is awful - only a photo.') to furious provocation and threats ('Come on, damn you, ring me. Or else.') culminates in crushing impotence ('What?/ I don't know what.'). The lonely final line drifts away from the poem, as disconnected and vulnerable as the speaker, leaving the poem to reach the same dead end the speaker does. It is a devastatingly pithy yet pitiful line, pathos epitomised. More optimistically, writing the poem at least gives the speaker an attentive listener: the reader. No more can Kay do for that tortured soul.

CRUNCHing The Phone:

WORST - LOVE - BEST - DISASTER - SIRENS - NOBODY - FUTURE - MARRIAGE - STRANGER'S - TRY - ASSAULT - RE-READ - WAITING - SILVER - EXTRA - INFURIATINGLY - BORING - LONELY - TRAPPED - AWFUL - RING - DON'T

Simon Armitage, *Remains*

According to Judith Lewis Herman, 'the conflict between the will to deny horrible events and the will to proclaim them aloud is the central dialectic of psychological trauma'. It is this trauma that is undeniably at the heart of Armitage's poem. Originally published in the 2008 collection 'The Not Dead', *Remains* is one of a series of poems that seek to understand and convey the mentality of British soldiers after returning from wars overseas. Based on actual interviews with three returned soldiers, Armitage observed that 'most of the poems I wrote revolved around a key 'flashback' scene, requiring each soldier to revisit the very incident he was desperately hoping to forget' and it is easy to see the marks of Post-Traumatic Stress Disorder within *Remains* as the soldier struggles to come to terms with the fallout of taking a life.

We get sent out

We join our speaker mid-conversation, in what first appears to be another casual tale in a series of stories. We have no idea what's come before – we are thrown into the story *in media res* – which is important both because it reflects the significance of this particular moment to the soldier, and also because it denies the reader the opportunity to understand the context of the situation. We, like the soldier later reveals himself to be, are trapped in this moment, and can only draw out meaning from the images presented to us.

At first glance, it is easy to dismiss the soldier's anecdotal opening and conversational tone as evidence that conflict and violence have become normalised, everyday things to the speaker – after all, this is simply 'another occasion'. The soldier's speech is composed of casual, off-hand and colloquial language; hence it appears that this is just another story to tell down the pub. He talks of how they 'get sent out', of 'one of his mates', of shooting, euphemistically, as 'letting fly', of a body being 'carted off'. Although we know that the speaker is really there to handle a potentially violent robbery, the use of the verb 'tackle' also lulls us into a false sense of familiarity. A word so heavily associated with sports such as football and rugby – with *games* – serves as another euphemism, distancing us emotionally from the brutal reality of the situation. The continued use of colloquial expressions such as 'legs it' and phrases that mimic the rhythm of conversation ('well myself and somebody else and somebody else') further obscures the harshness of what is really happening, to the point that it is genuinely shocking when the three soldiers 'open fire'. And the transition from ordinary to horrific happens so fast, in just a few lines into the poem, embodying in the verse the way the situation escalated suddenly. There is a sharp contrast between the ordinary, conversational tone and the extreme violence of the situation, a sense that this is just another day at the office and the soldier is completely divorced from, perhaps numbed by, the reality of his actions.

This impression is reinforced by the callous way in which the soldier describes the treatment of the body afterwards. The looter is treated with a shocking lack of respect that likens him to rubbish; there is no moment of consideration for the fact that the soldiers have just taken a human life. Instead, one of them simply 'tosses his guts back into his body' and the looter is then 'carted off in the back of a lorry'. The looter is seemingly easily disposable, just a bit of rubbish, the speaker's use of colloquial verbs such as 'tossed' and 'carted off' imply an everyday occurrence. Violence has become normalised and human life has become devalued – the soldier simply no longer cares. Notice too how that telling phrase about whether the looter was 'probably armed, possibly not' is repeated in the poem. It's a crucial detail; did the soldiers mow down an unarmed man or not? But the verse passes swiftly over it, as if this crucial legal and moral question is almost an irrelevance.

Near the knuckle

Whilst the first half of the poem makes it easy to dismiss the speaker as an unfeeling cog in the war machine, and to chalk the poem up to yet another commentary on the harsh reality of conflict, the final four stanzas clearly show the long-lasting effects this traumatic event has on the soldier's psyche. Haunted by the looter's death, the soldier's own life seems to come to a standstill, forever locked in a nightmare moment he cannot escape. The true tragedy here is not that the soldier does not feel guilt, but that he is unable to articulate or process his feelings.

Trauma is paradoxical in nature – there is a tension between the constant return to the repressed (or unwanted) memory and the inability to fully express it in a way that renders it whole. In Remains, the soldier is trapped in the horror of the moment, but never able to truly convey his feelings. He lacks the vocabulary that would allow him to express himself, instead falling back on more familiar colloquial phrases from everyday life. The references to sport ('tackle') and poker ('three of a kind') are not meant to suggest that the speaker sees war as a game. Instead, they show his inability to fully comprehend and process what has happened – he must relate the terrible events of that day to safer, more recognisable experiences.

Armitage's poem is a dramatic monologue and there are, notably, almost two voices within the poem. The calm, conversational, surface voice speaks with mostly informal phrases. Concurrently, underneath it, between the lines is a starker, more emotional voice that expresses the soldier's true revulsion. This is most clearly heard in the second and third stanzas, where the recollection of the actual shooting seems to throw the speaker into a horrifying flashback. Whilst casually introduced with the colloquial phrasing of 'three of a kind all letting fly', the fallout of the soldier's actions is initially expressed through a violent metaphor that shockingly jars with the tone of the first two stanzas. Suddenly, the violence becomes all too real: 'I see every round as it rips through his life'. The language here is brutally clear; a string of monosyllabic words full of sharp consonants, the alliterative 'r's' echoing the ripping apart of both the looter's and the soldier's lives, the single plosive 'p' imitating the sound of a single gunshot. The horror of the memory is overwhelming. Almost immediately, the soldier retreats into the familiarity of his casual phrasing: 'so we've hit this looter a dozen times'. His description of the man's body being 'sort of inside out' is almost childish, the addition of the hedge, 'sort of', clearly reflecting his inability to express himself, yet this makes it even more horrific.

End of

The opening line of the fifth stanza is also brutal, but this time in its tone of bitter irony. One of the few sentences that remains contained within a single line, with a full stop at the end, its real purpose is to show us that, despite his determination to put the incident squarely behind him, this story can never truly end for the soldier. The looter's life is over. The soldier's mission is over. But the soldier will never be able to fully escape the memories of what he has done. This is the volta, the turning point of the poem. Here we begin to fully realise the long-lasting, traumatic wound these events have made upon the soldier.

The 'blood-shadow' of the looter 'stays on the street', something that the soldier must 'walk right over [...] week after week'. Whilst this image serves as a neat visual reminder of the man's death, it also mirrors how the soldier will be haunted by his memories. The repetition of 'week after week' creates the illusion of an endless amount of time, foreshadowing the years that the soldier will suffer, whilst the compression of the two nouns clearly and concisely demonstrates the effect the looter's death will have upon the soldier. Just as a shadow constantly follows us wherever we go, so too will the soldier be haunted by the guilt he feels and the metaphorical blood on his hands.

Armitage further emphasises this lingering trauma by immediately following the image of the 'blood-shadow' with the soldier's return 'home on leave'. Whilst the short, simple sentence, ending mid-line, suggests that the soldier optimistically thinks that the 'story' will end with his return home and he'll be able to forget about it, the reality is near instantly revealed. To the soldier's horror, he only has to 'blink /and he bursts again through the doors of the bank'. The flashback is harsh and sudden; the plosive alliteration in 'But I blink', 'bursts' and 'bank' highlights the explosive force of the memory. The effect is enhanced by the preceding caesura, which emphasises the suddenness of its onset. From one 'blink' to the next, the soldier is helplessly caught in his own memory, the enjambment reflecting the horror he cannot escape; just as the line continues across the two stanzas, the memory of the looter's death has followed the soldier home.

Armitage's soldier clearly cannot cope with the memory of his actions, torn apart by his inner turmoil in much the same way as the looter was 'torn apart by a dozen rounds'. Trapped in his own memories, he is doomed to endlessly repeat the events of that day, as is shown through the poem's almost cyclical nature. The images of the bank, the ripped apart body and the 'dozen' shots from the first half of the poem are repeated, as is the line 'probably armed, possibly not'. The soldier is haunted by possibilities, constantly going over and trying to justify his actions. Even the penultimate line, 'but near to the knuckle, here and now' maintains the same rhythm as 'probably armed, possibly not', suggesting that there is no escape from these distressing memories for the soldier, even by the end of the poem.

Whilst the desperate admittance that the 'drinks and the drugs won't flush him out' is by itself a tragic confession of the soldier's state of mind, the use of the word 'flush' – a word often associated with hunting, and the flushing out of prey – suggests that the soldier has become truly vulnerable and is unable to process and control his violent memories. The looter is 'dug in behind enemy lines', a metaphor for how the memory of his death refuses to be brushed away. Once again, the soldier can only articulate his emotions in familiar phrases; however, here he must fall back on the language of soldiery rather than colloquial sayings, perhaps hinting that the soldier's traumatic flashbacks are increasingly distancing him from the normal and every day.

Superficially the poem looks orderly, regular and composed. Seven fairly even quatrains finish with a final neat couplet. Examine it more closely, however and this appearance of control is revealed to be misleading. Take the rhyming, for instance: Though rhymes do crop up in the poem from time to time, often in pairs ('round'/'ground'; 'myself'/'somebody else'; 'mind'/'times') and sometimes in triplets ('street'/'weeks'/'sleep') they appear in odd, unexpected places, as if the rhyme pattern has been knocked askew. This impression is enhanced by the frequent use of pararhymes, such as 'lorry'/'story' and 'blink'/'bank'. Add to this the lack of a regular governing metre and it becomes clear that the impression of control and composure is superficial and only partly hides the internal disarray. Clearly too this pattern embodies the impression the soldier gives of himself. Outwardly he might appear to be fine, but internally things are very different indeed.

Gradually, as we progress through the poem, we see, in fact, how the soldier loses more and more control – slowly, at first, but then with ever increasing rapidity. With particularly traumatic moments highlighted through plosives and dashes right from the start, moments of terror breaking through the faux-casual control of the soldier's words, the pacing of the poem picks up after the soldier returns home on leave. The poem ends with one single continuous sentence that runs for seven lines, across three stanzas, a constant stream of enjambment that expresses the soldier's ongoing pain and the endless repetition of his flashbacks. The list of sibilant adjectives describing the 'distant, sun-stunned, sand-smothered land' is nearly explosive. Violent compound adjectives convey the soldier's state of mind and how he himself feels suffocated by his memories. Like the unusually long line, the speaker's own mind is unravelling and losing control. By the end of the poem, the standard four-line stanza format has been shattered and the poem concludes in a simple non-rhymed couplet, representing the fracturing of the soldier's own sense of self.

And somebody else and somebody else

Armitage set out to explore the effect of war on soldiers and *Remains* clearly succeeds in showing the destruction war wreaks upon those who participate in it. Even the title is as divided. Clearly it refers to the human remains of the looter, but also too to how this memory remains in the psyche of the soldier. Moreover, the title suggests that the soldier is himself also now missing some part of himself; he is also the remains of this brutal experience. And this unnamed soldier is an everyman figure. Armitage could have added specific details to tie this story to a specific war, such as the Iraq war. The fact that he doesn't signals that he wanted to get at something universal about the experience of conflict. The anonymous narrator thus embodies the way in which abuse and trauma is passed on and carried over from one situation to another.

Whilst the cyclical nature of the poem embodies his inability to escape his memories, it is also notable that the entire poem is told in present tense. Hence the soldier is also trapped in one moment in time, unable to put in the past and move on. Nowhere is this clearer than in the third stanza, where Armitage's use of anaphora highlights how the trauma is ongoing for the speaker. By repeating 'I see' at the beginning of the two lines, the poet emphasises the pain and horror of the moment, showing that it is a vision that can never go away.

The poem takes on a confessional air. There is a distinct sense that the speaker sets out to comfort himself by sharing blame. Beginning with the first-person plural 'we' suggests collective responsibility. It is not the soldier alone who decided to shoot: it is 'myself and somebody else and somebody else', who are explicitly described as being 'all of the same mind'. Repetitive listing implies a desperation to share the responsibility for his actions, further emphasised by the almost superfluous repetition of 'all' no less than three times in a single stanza. But as soon as the shots have been fired, the narrative switches to the first-person singular 'I'. With the exception of a single 'we've', the rest of the poem focuses exclusively on the speaker and his own personal guilt, culminating as the soldier finds himself completely responsible for the man's death: 'his bloody life in my bloody hands'.

His bloody life in my bloody hands

There are echoes of Lady Macbeth here, haunted to madness by guilt and the metaphorical blood on her hands; a particularly striking image that ends the poem. Earlier still, we are reminded of Macbeth after the murder of Duncan with the emphasis placed on 'Sleep' and 'Dream' in the sixth stanza. Both words begin their respective lines, separated by caesurae, lending them focus. Just as Macbeth's violent actions 'doth murder sleep', so too do the soldier's. These emphasised words can even be linked to Hamlet's famous soliloquy as he muses over whether 'to sleep, perchance to dream'. The Danish prince's reflections over the afterlife and what awaits us there seem a remarkably apt concern for the soldier. With such a vivid sense of tragedy in *Remains*, it is easy to see the after-images of these characters within Armitage's traumatised soldier, and how they remain with him. If he can share nothing else with his victim, he shares the blood and, in the poem's final couplet, looter and soldier are fused

Inseparably together.

Although Armitage vividly depicts the brutal effects of conflict, this is not a poem dedicated to attacking the idea of war. Instead, it invites us to empathise with those who fight and to try to understand what they must live with. The soldier's colloquial phrasing, with his chatty tone and frequent use of contractions, draws us in and allows us to connect with his thought processes in a way that is perhaps impossible with the more rigidly controlled structures of other conflict poetry. Armitage's soldier develops an authentic voice that we can recognise. He is a real and, most importantly, human insight into the realities of war and its after-effects. As Armitage points out, 'for traumatized soldiers, the harrowing images and accompanying feelings persist, in some cases for a lifetime.' This poem does not judge the soldier's actions as right or wrong; what it does is allow us to gain that little bit of extra insight into this eternal issue.

Remains crunched:

TACKLE – LEGS IT – PROBABLY – POSSIBLY – ALL – I – RIPS – LOOTER – DOZEN – AGONY – TOSSES – GUTS – CARTED OFF – STORY – BLOOD-SHADOW – BLINK – BURSTS – SLEEP – FLUSH – HEAD – DUG IN – ENEMY – SUN-STUNNED – SAND-SMOTHERED – BLOODY

Eve L Ewing, *Origin Story*

Super-poet

It's notoriously difficult to eke out a living as a writer, particularly so if you're a poet. Consequently, many writers do other jobs alongside their writing. Not many, however, have second jobs as busy, exciting or glamorous as the American poet Eve L. Ewing. As well as working as visual artist, and in academia as a sociologist, and as an activist supporting youth arts education programmes, Ewing has recently been commissioned to write stories for Marvel comics. The writer of the 'Ironheart' comics from 2018, in 2023 she became the first black female author of the celebrated 'Black Panther' series and in 2024 she also began writing stories for the 'X-Men' comics. Perhaps then, it's not surprising that as well as featuring an extended celebration of comic books as a metaphor for love, the title and subject of her prose poem, *Origin Story* echoes a key narrative trope of superhero narratives - the story of the superhero's past and how they discovered their superpowers. Hence, through this wry intertextual reference, with a winning touch of humour, Ewing's poem suggests that the poet herself is a kind of superhero, the 'good ending' to her parent's marriage.

The dynamic duo

Ostensibly, the central narrative in *Origin Story* explores, however, the messy complexity of love. The poem describes the love story of the speaker's parents, from the moment that they met, by accident or fate, at a bus station, to the conclusion of their relationship. Ewing explores the impermanence of love, and yet how this fragility does not prevent it from being memorable and meaningful. Whilst some love stories do not last forever, the poet suggests, they can still have a deep and lasting impact.

The first stanza begins with an exploration of how the speaker's parents met. The 'Greyhound bus station' is a significant detail. Since a bus station is a place of transition, this location suggests how the parents' own lives had been separate and unsettled prior to their meeting and it also foreshadows, perhaps, the temporary nature of their relationship. In the States, Greyhound buses and their bus station are also associated with the Civil Rights movement, adding a political resonance to this setting. The parents' identities are celebrated through the descriptions of their youthful qualities. Her mother's 'Afropuff', for instance, references a popular style for Afro hair, and alongside her performance in a 'Chaka Khan cover band', is symbolic of Black identity. The fact that she was in a cover band, however, may also show that her mother was still in the process of discovering her own sense of self when she met the speaker's father; she was experimenting with other artists' songs rather than writing her own. Her father, in contrast, is presented less as stylish and more as serious-minded; we are told he 'mimeographed communist newspapers', conveying his political orientation and commitments as a young man, qualities inherited by the poet.[3] There is a hint here of her father's youth, and, perhaps, a subtle suggestion that he may have been more intent focus on radical politics rather than on the commitment needed for a long-term relationship. The cultural references also suggest the connections between personal stories and wider social movements, and these details convey the speaker's pride in her parents' identities, her celebration of individuality and artistic and political freedom.

---

[3] Many of Ewing's poems overtly confront racial prejudice and historical injustices. Her collection, '1919', for instance, explores the notorious race riots of that year.

Love is a comic book

Unlike Shakespeare, who famously compared his love to a summer's day, this poet uses the innovative and entertaining extended metaphor of a comic book to convey love as something both precious and fallible. The speaker's father 'drew comic books/ like this one, for sale. one dollar./ my mother bought one.' The caesura here disrupts the rhythm of the line, creating a short pause, like an intake of breath, suggesting the significance of this meeting between the speaker's mother and father, and how this unexpected discovery of love disrupted the rhythm of their lives. The fragmented sentence 'one dollar' not only invites readers to understand the father's need for money, but perhaps also shows the lack of worth attributed to the art he produced. Historically, comic book art tended to be dismissed snobbishly by serious art critics as second rate and beneath their attention, at least up until artists such as Roy Lichtenstein produced artworks based on comic book images. A comic book is something that can be seen as trivial and unimportant, a piece of cultural ephemera that may be undervalued and given away all too easily. Of course, as we have read, for this poet, comic books are far more important than that, not least because they are another special interest inherited from her father. Whilst the transaction of the purchasing of a comic book is seemingly insignificant, the end-stopping after 'dollar' and 'one' also highlights that this moment marked a turning point: the ending of their individual youthful lives, and the beginning of their relationship together. It could, alternatively, be a foreshadowing of the temporary nature of their relationship, one that was not destined to go on.

The image of the comic book is carried into the second stanza, where the literal object takes on a more metaphorical meaning. As the speaker reflects, 'love is like a comic book', a simile that the poet quotes and then riffs on and that encapsulates the thematic heart of the poem; falling in love is exhilarating, joyful and playful, but also makes us vulnerable, and love is not always destined to last. The line at the start of the second stanza is not capitalised. This stylistic choice subverts expectations – as much of Ewing's work does – by challenging grammatical conventions.

Perhaps the simile also suggests that love is sometimes insubstantial. The poem shifts in tone in this second stanza from the narrative structure of its first stanza to a more abstract reflection on the nature of love. Love is 'fragile' and although it is 'never meant to last', it is like a stray animal that 'might find its way to another decade, another home, an attic, a basement, intact'. The listing here highlights that love is something is persistent and resilient and can crop up in unexpected places, but also that it needs to be looked after. The use of enjambment, additionally, suggests that, with hard work and nurture, a relationship can blossom and does not have to reach a dead-end. Like a comic, however, a relationship can easily be discarded or torn apart if not treated with care. The metaphor 'love is paper', in a short, end-stopped line in the middle of the second stanza, reminds readers of the multifaceted nature of love: Delicate, like paper, it is also precious, and, like paper, has the potential to last if we 'protect' it properly.

Without a metre, a rhyme scheme or clear lineation, *Origin Story* is the most radical sort of free verse poem, a prose poem. Sometimes it is presented as a series of paragraphs, at others it is arranged in two stanzas, more like a conventional poem. However, even in this second manifestation, the stanzas are irregular, and the use of free verse structurally suggests the unpredictability of love, particularly in the case of youthful relationships. In both formats, the irregular structure also reflects the complex nature of life itself, as something complex and changeable; inevitably, some moments or relationships last longer than others. In addition, perhaps this form fits an origin story that has unfolded in an irregular, unconventional way.

To create pathways toward that which we have never seen, we have to lead with imagination

In the poetry format, the second stanza is the longer of the two, and it returns to a focus on the relationship between the speaker's parents, reminding readers that this poem is a personal reflection. ('This is true', the speaker tells us in the opening line, suggesting that stories can hold truths and memories that last far longer than the paper that contains them). The love between her parents did not receive the care that it needed. It 'never saw polyvinyl', for example, an image that suggests it was never properly protected or valued. Worse, it was 'mishandled, worn thin' so that it 'rusted'. The listing implies that their relationship had to endure their youthful behaviour, possible unfaithfulness ('lent to a friend') and a lack of care or attention ('never felt a backing'), as love was taken for granted. Rather than being cherished, this precious love seems to have been passed around casually, even left, forgetfully, like a comic, 'over the back of a couch'. The ending of the poem, instilled with nostalgia, reminds readers that this is not a meditation on a failed relationship, but rather, one that was perhaps not meant to last forever, but was still romantic, valuable and, moreover, productive. The love story of the speaker's parents 'doesn't last/ but it has a good ending'. Enjambment here suggests that their love, and their lives, were fluid and unplanned, while the finality of the last line implies that the ending of their relationship was amicable.

Wittily, Ewing subverts the superhero origin stories, familiar from comic books and, latterly, films, by making her own belated, but disembodied appearance in the poem's last line. Rather than announcing herself with some kind of fanfare, the poet uses very ordinary, everyday phrasing to make this momentous event seem unremarkable, while the oblique way of referencing herself, makes her origin seem almost incidental to the main narrative. Nearly going under the radar, her appearance is, in fact, something an inattentive reader could easily miss. And in another subversion of these narratives, modestly, there's no mention at all of how the poet discovered her miraculous superpowers.

Origin Story (the prose format) crunched:

TRUE — MOTHER – 19 – BAND – FATHER – COMMUNIST –
BOUGHT – LOVE – CLUMSY – LAST – INTACT – PAPER –
BACKING – LENT – RUSTED – ENDING

'Poetry is everywhere; it just needs editing.'

JAMES TATE

A sonnet of revision activities

1. Reverse millionaire: 10,000 points if students can guess the poem just from one word from it. You can vary the difficulty as much as you like. For example, 'Communist', would be fairly easily identifiable as from Ewing's poem whereas 'clumsy' would be more difficult. 1000 points if students can name the poem from a single phrase or image – e.g. 'Oh what sweet company'. 100 points for a single line. 10 points for recognising the poem from a stanza. Play individually or in teams.

2. Research the poet. Find one sentence about them that you think sheds light on their poem in the anthology. Compare with your classmates. Or find a couple more lines or a stanza by a poet and see if others can recognise the writer from their lines. Is there anything distinctive about the way they write? Who, for instance, is this: 'The ancient pulse and germ and birth/ was shrunken hard and dry'?

3. Write a cento based on one or more of the poems. A cento is a poem constructed from lines from other poems. Difficult, creative, but also fun, perhaps.

4. Read 3 or 4 other poems by one of the poets. Write a pastiche. See if classmates can recognise the poet you're imitating.

5. Write the introduction for a critical guide on the poems aimed at next year's yr. 10 class.

6. Use the poet Glynn Maxwell's typology of poems to arrange the poems into different groups. In his excellent book, 'On Poetry', Maxwell suggests poems have four dominant aspects, which he calls solar, lunar, musical and visual. A solar poem hits home, is immediately striking. A lunar poem, by contrast, is more mysterious and might not give up its meanings so easily. Ideally a lunar poem will haunt your imagination. Written mainly for the ear, a musical poem focuses on the sounds of language, rather than

the meanings. Think of Lewis Carroll's *Jabberwocky*. A visual poem is self-conscious about how it looks to the eye. Concrete poems are the ultimate visual poems. According to Maxwell, the very best poems are strong in each dimension. Try applying this test to each poem. Which ones come out on top?

7. Maxwell also recommends conceptualising the context in which the words of the poem are created or spoken. Which poems would suit being read around a campfire? Which would be better declaimed from the top of a tall building? Which might you imagine read on a stage? Which ones are more like conversation overheard? Which are the easiest and which the most difficult to place?

8. Mr Maxwell is a fund of interesting ideas. He suggests all poems dramatise a battle between the forces of whiteness and blackness, nothingness and somethingness, sound and silence, life and death. In each poem, what is the dynamic between whiteness and blackness? Which appears to have the upper hand?

9. Still thinking in terms of evaluation, consider the winnowing effect of time. Which of the modern poems do you think might be still read in 20, a 100, or 200 years? Why?

10. Give yourself only the first and last line of one of the poems. Without peeking at the original, try to fill in the middle. Easy level: write in prose. Expert level: attempt verse.

11. According to Russian Formalist critics, poetry performs a 'controlled explosion on ordinary language'. What evidence can you find in this selection of controlled linguistic detonations?

12. A famous musician once said that though he wasn't the best at playing all the notes, nobody played the silences better. The sound of a water drop in Japanese garden water features is designed to make us notice the silence around it. Try reading one of the poems in the light of these comments, focusing on the use of white space, caesuras, punctuation – all the devices that create

the silence on which the noise of the poem rests.

13. In *Notes on the Art of Poetry*, Dylan Thomas wrote that 'the best craftsmanship always leaves holes and gaps in the works of the poem so that something that is not in the poem can creep, crawl, flash or thunder in'. Examine a poem in the light of this comment, looking for its holes and gaps. If you discover these, what 'creeps', 'crawls' or 'flashes' in to fill them?

14. Different types of poems conceive the purpose of poetry differently. Broadly speaking Augustan poets of the eighteenth century aimed to impress their readers with the wit of their ideas and the elegance of the expression. In contrast, Romantic poets wished to move their readers' hearts. Characteristically, more earnest Victorian poets aimed to teach the readers some kind of moral principle or example. Self-involved, avant-garde Modernists weren't overly bothered about finding, never mind pleasing, a general audience, they were too busy colliding fragments together, making linguistic collages. What impact do the Eduqas anthology poems seek? Do they seek to amuse, appeal to the heart, teach us something? Are they like soliloquies – the overheard inner workings of thinking – or more like speeches or mini-plays? Try placing each poem somewhere on the following continuums. Then create a few continuums of your own. As ever, comparison with your classmates will prove illuminating.

Emotional...intellectual
Feelings...ideas
Internal...external
Contemplative..rhetorical
Open...guarded

Terminology task

The following is a list of poetry terminology and short definitions of the terms. Unfortunately, cruel, malicious individuals [i.e. us] have scrambled them up. Your task is to unscramble the list, matching each term to the correct definition. Good luck!

Term	Definition
Imagery	Vowel rhyme, e.g. 'bat' and 'lag'
Metre	An implicit comparison in which one thing is said to be
Rhythm	another
Simile	Description in poetry
Metaphor	A conventional metaphor, such as a 'dove' for peace
Symbol	A metrical foot comprising an unstressed followed by a
Iambic	stressed beat
Pentameter	A line with five beats
Enjambment	Description in poetry using metaphor, simile or
Caesura	personification
Dramatic monologue	A repeated pattern of ordered sound
Figurative imagery	An explicit comparison of two things, using 'like' or 'as'
Onomatopoeia	Words, or combinations of words, whose sounds mimic their
Lyric	meaning
Adjective	Words in a line starting with the same letter or sound
Alliteration	A strong break in a line, usually signalled by punctuation
Ballad	A regular pattern of beats in each line
Sonnet	A narrative poem with an alternating four and three beat line
Assonance	A word that describes a noun
Sensory imagery	A 14-line poem following several possible rhyme schemes
Quatrain	When a sentence steps over the end of a line and continues
Diction	into the next line or stanza
Personification	Description that uses the senses
	A four-line stanza
	Inanimate objects given human characteristics
	A poem written in the voice of a character
	A poem written in the first person, focusing on the emotional
	experience of the narrator
	A term to describe the vocabulary used in a poem

Comparing the poems

There will be many ways in which these poems could be compared, of course, and often it is as helpful to focus on differences as much as similarities. The poems could be compared in terms of their use of devices such as metaphors or via their formal features. However, probably the most useful and productive way to compare them is through how they handle their major themes. The following is a suggested, but not exhaustive, list of possibilities for thematic comparison.

Nature

An obvious pairing in the collection is the that of the poems by the two Williams, the Romantic poets Blake and Wordsworth. Eduqas tends to ask thematic questions and clearly both these poems are about the relationships between man and nature. The intense feelings both poets express about nature have many things in common; in both *The Schoolboy* and *I Wandered Lonely as a Cloud* nature is a source of beauty, joy and comfort and both poets contrast these feelings with more negative ones. Blake's poem compares the freedom of communing with nature with harsh and opressive schooling, while Wordsworth finds comfort in recalling his vision of daffodils during less happy moments. McKay's poem, *I Shall Return*, could be compared interestingly with either of these poems, with the natural world again celebrated and the speaker feeling intense desire to escape to it as a form of sanctuary. Additionally, Heaney's poem, *Blackberry-Picking* also features a strong and intimate relationship with the natural world. The darker undercurrents that develop in Heaney's poem could be compared to the feelings of exile in McKay's or oppression in Blake's or of pensive unease in Wordsworth's. Meanwhile, Heaney and Blake's poems both feature child narrators.

Love & relationships

Sonnet 29 and *Cousin Kate* are both poems about love and relationships, but present very different situations. The overwhelming feeling of genuine love Barrett Browning's enraptured speaker expresses is very different to the lust that drives the exploitation of the young girl in Rossetti's poem. Jackie Kay's poem *Dusting the Phone* could be compared with *Sonnet*

29 in terms of the pleasures and pains of being in love and especially the longing for an absent lover. **Catrin** and **Origin Story** could be compared to any of these three poems, as both focus on signficant relationships, albeit in *Catrin* of a mother and her daughter, rather than between lovers. Both *Catrin* and *Origin Story* explore relationships between parents and children, but, whereas Clarke presents this from a parental perspective, Ewing does so from that of the child. Whereas Clarke describes her daughter, Ewing describes her parents.

The Pity of War

Another clear grouping in the anthology is poems about warfare, particularly the aftermath of fighting. **Drummer Hodge** and **Disabled** both present us with innocent victims or war, young men, not much more than boys, who suffered horribly and who did not really know what they were letting themselves in for. In both poems we feel the pity of war, but, whereas the emotions are understated in Hardy's poem, they are expressed with more direct bitterness in Owen's. **Remains** and **Kamikaze** also deal with the after effects of warfare, but in different ways to the first two. Written in the first person, Armitage's poem presents things from the perspective of a perpetrator of violence, rather than a victim, although as the poem unfolds we realise the speaker has become both. Similarly, Garland's poem focuses on what happens after the fighitng has finished, the damgage done to close relationships, such as the mother not speaking to her father after the war. Like *Disabled*, *Kamikaze* is also structured on a contrast between before and after the experience of fighting in wars.

The suffering of others

Decomposition and **War Photographer** both explore reactions to the suffering of others and the responsibilites we all have as witnesses. In particular, both poems express ambivalent feelings of the two photographers and suggest the potential danger of exploitating other people's suffering, intetionally or inadvertently, for our own ends.

Growing up

The main theme of Heaney's poem, **Blackberry-Picking**, is the speaker's development from innocence to experience, from childish perspectives on the world to more complex adult ones. In addition to offering productive comparison to the nature poems, Heaney's poem could be compared with

Clarke's *Catrin*, which presents the theme of growing up and change from a different perspective, that of a mother rather than that of a child. Ewing's poem, *Origin Story*, approaches the same theme, though more obliquely.

GLOSSARY

ALLITERATION – the repetition of consonants at the start of neighbouring words in a line

ANAPAEST - a three-beat pattern of syllables, unstress, unstress, stress. E.g. 'on the moon', 'to the coast', 'anapaest'

ANTITHESIS - the use of balanced opposites

APOSTROPHE – a figure of speech addressing a person, object or idea

ASSONANCE – vowel rhyme, e.g. sod and block

BLANK VERSE – unrhymed lines of iambic pentameter

BLAZON – a male lover describing the parts of his beloved

CADENCE – the rise of fall of sounds in a line of poetry

CAESURA – a distinct break in a poetic line, usually marked by punctuation

COMPLAINT – a type of love poem concerned with loss and mourning

CONCEIT – an extended metaphor

CONSONANCE – rhyme based on consonants only, e.g. book and back

COUPLET – a two-line stanza, conventionally rhyming

DACTYL – the reverse pattern to the anapaest; stress, unstress, unstress. E.g. 'Strong as a'

DRAMATIC MONOLOGUE – a poem written in the voice of a distinct character

ELEGY – a poem in mourning for someone dead

END-RHYME – rhyming words at the end of a line

END-STOPPED – the opposite of enjambment; i.e. when the sentence and the poetic line stop at the same point

ENJAMBMENT – where sentences run over the end of lines and stanzas

FIGURATIVE LANGUAGE – language that is not literal, but employs figures of speech, such as metaphor, simile and personification

FEMININE RHYME – a rhyme that ends with an unstressed syllable or unstressed syllables.

FREE VERSE – poetry without metre or a regular, set form

GOTHIC – a style of literature characterised by psychological horror, dark deeds and uncanny events

HEROIC COUPLETS – pairs of rhymed lines in iambic pentameter

HYPERBOLE – extreme exaggeration

IAMBIC – a metrical pattern of a weak followed by a strong stress, ti-TUM, like a heartbeat

IMAGERY – the umbrella term for description in poetry. Sensory imagery refers to descriptions that appeal to sight, sound and so forth; figurative imagery refers to the use of devices such as metaphor, simile and personification

JUXTAPOSITION – two things placed together to create a strong contrast

LYRIC – an emotional, personal poem usually with a first-person speaker

MASCULINE RHYME – an end rhyme on a strong syllable

METAPHOR – an implicit comparison in which one thing is said to be another

METAPHYSICAL – a type of poetry characterised by wit and extended metaphors

METRE – the regular pattern organising sound and rhythm in a poem

MOTIF – a repeated image or pattern of language, often carrying thematic significance

OCTET OR OCTAVE – the opening eight lines of a sonnet

ONOMATOPOEIA – bang, crash, wallop

PENTAMETER – a poetic line consisting of five beats

PERSONIFICATION – giving human characteristics to inanimate things

PLOSIVE – a type of alliteration using 'p' and 'b' sounds

QUATRAIN – a four-line stanza

REFRAIN – a line or lines repeated like a chorus

ROMANTIC – A type of poetry characterised by a love of nature, by strong emotion and heightened tone

SESTET – the last six lines in a sonnet

SIMILE – an explicit comparison of two different things

SONNET – a form of poetry with fourteen lines and a variety of possible set rhyme patterns

SPONDEE – two strong stresses together in a line of poetry

STANZA – the technical name for a verse

SYMBOL – something that stands in for something else. Often a concrete representation of an idea.

SYNTAX – the word order in a sentence. doesn't Without sense English syntax make. Syntax is crucial to sense: For example, though it uses all the same words, 'the man eats the fish' is not the same as 'the fish eats the man'

TERCET – a three-line stanza

TETRAMETER – a line of poetry consisting of four beats

TROCHEE – the opposite of an iamb; stress, unstress, strong, weak.

VILLANELLE – a complex interlocking verse form in which lines are recycled

VOLTA – the 'turn' in a sonnet from the octave to the sestet

About the authors

Head of English, presenter and freelance writer, Neil Bowen has a Masters degree in Literature & Education from Cambridge University and is a member of Ofqual's experts panel for English. The co-author and editor of *The Art of Writing English Essays for A-level and Beyond* and of *The Art of Poetry*, *The Art of Drama* and *The Art of Literature* series. Neil runs the peripeteia project, bridging the gap between A-level and degree level English courses: peripeteia.co.uk

An Irish English teacher, Michael Meally has first class degrees in both English Literature and Engineering as well as a Masters degree in American Literature. Michael is the co-author of *The Art of Writing English Essays for A-level* and Beyond and has contributed to many of the books in *The Art of...* series.

Currently studying for a PhD focused on language, gender and identity Alice is an English teacher, writer and presenter. Alice has presented at various conferences, including at ResearchEd, UKLA and at NAWE.

With thanks to our other contributors, Karen Elson, Neil Jones & Kathrine Mortimore.